LOVE NOTES:

Everything is Love

An Anthology of African and East European Indigenous Languages

Volume 1

Curated and edited by Tendai Rinos Mwanaka

Mwanaka Media and Publishing Pvt Ltd,
Chitungwiza Zimbabwe
*
Creativity, Wisdom and Beauty

Publisher: *Mmap*
Mwanaka Media and Publishing Pvt Ltd
24 Svosve Road, Zengeza 1
Chitungwiza Zimbabwe
mwanaka@yahoo.com
mwanaka13@gmail.com
https://www.mmapublishing.org
www.africanbookscollective.com/publishers/mwanaka-media-and-
publishing
https://facebook.com/MwanakaMediaAndPublishing/

Distributed in and outside N. America by African Books Collective
orders@africanbookscollective.com
www.africanbookscollective.com

ISBN: 978-1-77925-584-6
EAN: 9781779255846

Table of Contents

iii

iv

V

vi

vii

About Editor

Tendai Rinos Mwanaka is a Zimbabwean publisher, editor, mentor, thinker and multidisciplinary artist with over 40 books published. He writes in English and Shona. His work has been nominated, shortlisted and won several prizes, that has also appeared in over 400 journals and anthologies from over 30 countries, and has been translated into Spanish, Shona, Serbian, Arabic, Bengali, Tamil, Macedonian, Albanian, Hungarian, Russian, Romanian, French and German. In another life, he is an avid gardener, cook, farmer, entrepreneur and marketer

Contributors Bio Notes

Balddine Moussa is a poet and artist born in the Comoros Islands. He has a strong passion for writing and art in general, and poetry in particular. Recently, the results of the call for proposals "Perception of China: our history of resistance to the epidermis", organized by the board of directors of the national fund for studies abroad and co-organized by the Chinese magazine Scholar have been published; only his article was retained in his school Zhejiang Normal University. His poems appear in *Best New African Poets, 2018, 2019, and 2020* editions as well as in `` Corpses of Unity. "

Kuleza John Lembi is a Malawian poet and actor, who is currently a final year medical student at College of Medicine, Malawi. He has written several English and Chichewa poems that are currently being aired on Malawi's radio and TV stations, some of his poems have been featured in Local newspapers and *Best New African Poets 2020 Anthology.* He is a contributor in the book "The wise fool" published in the year 2013. Currently he is the publicity and publications director of College of Medicine students' union.

Maria Filipova-Hadji - born in 1954 in the village of Sitovo, Burgas region - Bulgaria. She studied high school, economics school, Russian philology, journalism and Russian-Tatar philology in the cities of Sliven, Plovdiv and Tashkent-Uzbekistan. She is the editor of the first Bulgarian newspaper in Cyprus. She is the author of collections of poetry in Bulgarian and Greek, as well as collections of short stories in Bulgarian and Greek. She has translated poems, short stories, and children's stories from Greek into Bulgarian and Russian. She has participated in world, Greek and Russian poetic anthologies and short story collections (in Russia, Uzbekistan, Greece, Belgium, Peru, India, etc.). Her works have been translated into Greek, Russian, Uzbek, French, English, German, Spanish, Indian, and others. She is the author of the poetry books: "Butterfly Wing", "At the foot of dawn", "Crown for birds", a collection of poetry and prose, "Forgiveness for Bulgaria", "Between Strandzha and Florida"- a novel, "The Fourth

Pillar" - a novel, "Mother's Flowers" - stories and more. There are two books published in Greek that have no Bulgarian translation: "Ke den me affini o Teos") "And God does not leave me) - stories, as well as "Exomologisi" ("Confessions") - verses. Maria is a member of the Northern Greece Writers Union. One of the founders of "Cultural Bridge between Bulgaria and Uzbekistan" and "Art Residence in Uzbekistan" as coordinator for European countries.

Adrian SUCIU: He is considered one of the most important poets and journalists to stand out in Romania after the fall of the Communist regime. "Postponed Mythologies" (2011, poetry), "A Bullshit Novel" (2013, fiction), "The Popular Prophet" (2015, poetry), "Treaty of Walking on Waters" (2021, poetry) are among his published books. He is the president of the Cultural Media Branch of the Professional Journalists Union from Romania and a cultural TV programs-producer. He has been the president of the Cultural Association Direcția 9 since 2013, having promoted a large number of gifted young poets.

Seda Suna Uçakan: The Poet was born in 26th of May in 1983 in Ankara/Polatlı. She completed her primary school education in various cities of Turkey and her primary, elementary and high school education were completed in Bursa. She was graduated from Eskişehir Osmangazi University, the department of Comparative Literature and she still continues to study to get her master's degree in the same college. She works as an academic in her own field and she also works for a publishing house as an editress in İstanbul. Besides Turkish, her native language, she can also speak English and French. She continues her literary works by translating novels, poems and short stories from English and French. She believes that reading poems is crucial to write poems and she tries to understand the universe and convey its messages with her poems. Her poems and writings have been published in two international poetry antologies and various magazines and she has a poetry book called "Pay Sususları". Her poems have been translated to English, French, Indian. She lives in İstanbul/Turkey.

Borche Panov (1961, Radovish, North Macedonia) is a poet, essayist, dramaturge, an Arts Coordinator for the "International

Karamanov's Poetry Festival" held in Radovish annually for over 50 years, and Counselor for Culture and Education at the municipality of Radovish. He has been a member of the "Macedonian Writers' Association" since 1998, and has published 11 poetry books, 7 drama plays, and 5 books published in Macedonia, Bulgaria, Serbia, Slovenia and Croatia. His poetry was published in a number of anthologies, literary magazines and journals both at home and abroad, and his works are translated into many world languages.

Çağla Bölek was born in 1995 İstanbul, Turkey. She is an English Literature and Art Management graduate at Yeditepe University. Her English/Turkish poems have been published in *Natama Poetry and Criticism Magazine, Bosphorus Review of Books, Orlando, Veronika, Çamlık Magazine, Sanrı Zine, Sosyal Fanzine, Zerk Fanzine*. Her first poetic exhibition *creased; or cramped an experimentation in interplanary poetry* took place at *KargArt*. She also writes for arts, translates poetry and a regular performer at *İstanbul Poetry Slam*. She has a poetry band called *spiritus asper* where they merge poetry, music, and video-art.

Simbarashe Chirikure was born in 1974 at Musami Hospital, Murehwa District, Zimbabwe. He attended Zengeza 8 Primary School, and Zengeza 2 High School, Chitungwiza. He attained qualifications in Supervisory Management at Management Training Bureau, Masasa, and a Diploma in Business Leadership with the Zimbabwe Institute of Management. Some of his poetry is published in *Hodzeko Yenduri, Zimbolicious 3, Ngoma yeZimbabwe* and *Chitubu Chenduri* anthologies.

Daniela Andonovska-Trajkovska (1979, Bitola, Republic of North Macedonia) is poetess, scientist, editor of two literary magazines, literary critic, doctor of pedagogy, university professor, a member of the Macedonian Writers' Association, and a president of the Macedonian Science Society Editorial Council. She has published one prose book, 8 poetry books, literary critics, and over 100 scientific articles. She has won several important awards for literature such as "Krste Chachanski (2018), "Karamanov" (2019), Macedonian Literary Avant-garde (2020), "Abduvali Qutbiddin" (2020, Uzbekistan), Premio

Mondiale "Tulliola- Renato Filippelli" in Italy (2021) and "Aco Shopov" for poetry (by Macedonian Writers' Association in 2021).

Eldar Akhadov was born in Baku in 1960. He lives in Krasnoyarsk. A member of the Union of Writers of Russia and other writers 'organizations of Russia, Ukraine and Azerbaijan, a member of the Russian Geographical Society, Co-Chair of the Literary Council of the Assembly of Peoples of Eurasia, a member of the PEN International Writing Club. The author of 64 books of poetry and prose in Russian, English and Serbian. Laureate of the State Literary Prize of the Governor of the Yamal-Nenets Autonomous district, laureate of the National Prize "Silver Feather of Russia", "For the Good of the World", "North is a Country Without Borders", Silver medal of the IV All-Russian Literary Festival of Festivals, Silver medal of the IV Eurasia Literary Festival of Festivals. Winner of the competition "Best Book 2020" in the nomination "Books for Children and Youth".

Elena BĂLĂȘANU : She was born on 24th of November 1982, in Caracal. A graduate of the Faculty of Letters within the University of Craiova. She was awarded many literary prizes, among which the Special Award for an Oltenia-belonging author at the National Poetry Competition "Traian Demetrescu", Craiova, 2019 and the Great Prize at the National Poetry Competition "Panait Cerna", Tulcea, 2018. She published poetry in the literary magazines Mozaicul, Scrisul Românesc (Romanian Writing), Prăvălia culturală (The culture shop), Ateneu (Atheneum), Spații culturale (Cultural spaces), Ex Ponto, Bucovina Literară (Literary Bukovina), the literary sites O mie de semne (One thousand signs) and Noise Poetry, as well as the anthologies Caietele revistei „Sud" (The notebooks of the literay magazine "South") nr. 4/2005 and Literatura tânără (Young Literature) 2007, a collection carried out by Irina Petraș – Cluj-Napoca: Casa Cărții de Știință, 2007. She made her editorial debut with the poetry collection "Singurătatea nu ne face mai buni" ("Loneliness does not make us better"), Aius Publishing House, Craiova, 2020.

Eşref Ozan Baygın was born in 1993 in İstanbul. He graduated from Marmara University in the Biomedical Department and Anadolu University - International Relations. His poems have been published in Varlık Magazine, Statorec (Germany), Peyniraltı Edebiyatı, Bare of Dream (fanzine, Turkey) , Yazarkafa, Ankararınca, Orlando, At dergi, Edebiyatist, Akrostis (Belgium), Yeryüzü Düşleri, Americans and Others (anthology, Italy) and fanzines. Voice actor (Ne Nerede? - TGRT EU) His first poetry book, Kibrit Yanarken Bükülür, was published by Klaros Publications. His second poetry book, Piçin Yılı, was published by Sub Press. His works include "LSD OR COINCIDENCE," "PSYCHEDELIC POETRY" (Yazarkafa Magazine, no. 20), and "Beat Generation" (Yazarkafa Magazine, no. 22)

Joseph Daniel Sukali is a Malawian freelance writer, blogger, award winning spoken word poet and a mental health advocate. The 26 year old is a holder of a bachelor's degree obtained from Mzuzu University. Some of his works have been published in the *Best "New" African Poet 2020 Anthology*, Writers Global Movement (WGM) magazine, Mollywood Hip hop Magazine, the National and Times Newspaper just to mention a few.

Ruslan Pivovarov - Russian-language poet, born in Novomoskovsk, USSR/Ukraine in 1972, now lives in the city of Lida, Republic of Belarus. Member of the Belarusian Literary Union "Polotsk Branch". He has three published books of his poems. Multiple winner of many prestigious international literary competitions. Poems and prose have been published in more than twenty collective collections published by literary organizations in Russia, Ukraine, Germany, Tajikistan, Nepal, and Turkmenistan. In journals of Russia, Belarus, Ukraine, Syria, Greece, USA, Serbia, Turkmenistan. The author's poems and prose have been translated into 12 languages.

Göktürk Yaşar: He was born in 1997 in Bursa, Turkey. He is studying Philosophy at Istanbul University. In 2018, his poetry book named "Exile from Aden" was published. His poetry appeared in major magazines in Turkey. He lives in Bursa

Oscar Gwiriri is a Certified Forensic Investigations Professional (CFIP) who also holds a *Master of Science Degree in Strategic Management, Bachelor of Business Administration, Associate of Arts in Business Administration Degree, Diploma in Logistics and Transport (CILT,UK), Journeyman Class 1 Motor Mechanics* and *Diploma in Workplace Safety and Health*, as well as other ten certificates in the fraternity of United Nations Peacekeeping. He was born on 15 June 1975 in Zimbabwe. He so far has more than 30 publications both in English and Shona languages. He was nominated twice in the National Arts Merit Awards 2019 for his books *Hatiponi* and *Chitima nditakure*.

Marita Banda is a published writer and poet from Zambia. *Telling It Like It Is, a collection of eclectic poetry in English, French and Tumbuka* and *Traditional Zambian Etiquette for Modern Living* were published in 2017 and 2019. Her work has appeared in several publications including, *Of Shadows and Rainbow, Musings in Times of Covid*. She is co-founder of Sotrane Publishers, a subsidiary of the Network for Society Transformation, a civil society organisation that promotes use of favourable indigenous knowledge systems. Marita is the chairperson of the Zambia Reprographic Rights Society.

Nicoleta CRĂETE: She was born on 11th September, 1980, Romania. She has won numerous prizes, mainly for poetry, among which: 1st prize in the poetry section and the festival trophy at the Literature Festival Moştenirea Văcăreştilor in Târgovişte, 1st prize at the Poetry Competition Tudor Arghezi in Tg.-Jiu, in the section Bilete de Papagal, so on. Her debut volume, "The woman with a body of wax", was released in February 2019, at the Grinta Publishing House, in the collection Poezia 9, as a prize in the manuscript section of the International Poetry Festival from Sighetu Marmaţiei. The volume has also been awarded the Book of the Year Prize at the Ion Cănăvoiu Literature Festival in October 2019. Her poems have been translated into English, Czech, Spanish, French, Arabic, Hebrew. She is also a translator. Editor at Athanor.

Vesna Mundishevska-Veljanovska (1973, Bitola) is a member of the Macedonian Writers' Association, Macedonian Science Society –

Bitola and Bitola's Literary Circle. She is author of 13 books of poetry, 2 books of critical-essay texts, co-author of a book of poems for children and (co)author of 6 vocational books for teachers. Her poetry has been translated into many languages. She is represented in anthologies. She has won numerous poetry awards. She is editor of the Journal of Culture – Literature, Drama, Film and Publishing "Contemporary Dialogues", and has edited several journals of literature as well over forty poetry books and collections.

Ehoche Edache Elijah is a trained Biochemist (Mtech) from the federal University of Technology, Minna, Nigeria. A Christian based in his home country Nigeria, Elijah is fascinated with nature and this makes him a life student of nature. He has publications in sciences and poetry including Almajiri, the future of Africa, etc.

ZVONKO TANESKI, ASSOC. PROF. DR. (MACEDONIA / SLOVAKIA – born in 1980. He is a poet, literary translator and critic, redactor, anthologist, doctor of Philology, works as university professor at the Faculty of Philosophy, Comenius University in Bratislava. He is an ordinary member of the Independent Writers Club in Slovakia (since 2006), as well as of the Authors and Publicists International Association (APIA) with the seat in Riga – Latvia (since 2014); honorary member of the Slovak PEN Centre (since 2013) and a ordinary member since 2018, as well as member of several national and European artistic and scientific institutions, and scientific journals' editorial boards. He has received many literary and scientific rewards and acknowledgments in Macedonia and abroad, such as: C. R. I. C. For young artists of the Mediterranean and Balkan countries (Reggio Calabria, Italy, 1995), "Aco Karamanov" (Radovish, 1997), "Beli mugri" (Skopje, 2012), golden medal "Poet laureate" (Manilla – Philippines, 2013), the rector plaque for his literary and scientific work (Varna, Bulgaria, 2015), "Silver Flying Feather" by the Slavic Academy of Fine Arts and Literature (Varna, Bulgaria, 2018) etc. His books: "Open Gates" (1995), "The Choir of the Rotten Leafs" (2000), "Ridge" (2003), "Chocolates in Portfolio" (2010), "Tenderness without Warrant Paper" (2012) and "Waiting for the History" (2016). He has authored many linguistic papers and books. His work is published in more than 25 languages in approximately 30 countries in the world. He is writing poetry in Macedonian language exclusively

Obinna Chilekezi is a Nigerian poet of the Igbo tribe. His poems has appeared in journals and anthologies and he has five collections of poems. Chilekezi can be reached on ugobichi@yahoo.com and his Facebook handle is https://www.facebook.com/obinna.chilekezi.9

H.R.H. H.E. Pangeran Prince Love YM Dato Rdo. Sri Academician Amb. Prof. Dr. Kt Exp. GM LM Genius **Ivan Gaćina** was born on April 15, 1981 in Zadar, the Republic of Croatia. He writes poetry (including haiku), short stories, aphorisms, and book reviews. He is a member of many associations and societies. His work has been translated into several foreign languages, and he has received more than 200 awards at literary competitions, in his country and abroad. At the 9th International Photo-Haiku Contest "Setouchi-Matsuyama" in Japan, held in 2020, Ivan Gaćina won Grand Prix in the "Your Photo-Haiku in English" category, to which 542 photo-haiku with original photos of the sea were submitted.

Austin Kaluba is a journalist, poet, short story writer and translator. He studied Creative Writing at Oxford University (Department for continuing education) and University of Birkbeck in the UK. He was born in Zambia but is currently working in the UK.

Alfred Sunday Mukanaka: I'm a teacher by profession trained at the University of Zambia where I graduated in English and Literature. The talent for poetry was discovered in 1983 when my poem 'Arrival At Matumbo' was broadcast on BBC Arts and Africa. I have since then published a collection of poems in iCibemba, titled AMAKALATA (Letters). I have also ready, a manuscript for poems in English, some of which have appeared in the USA and local newspapers.

Abdulrahman M. Abu-Yaman is from the Nupe tribe predominantly around the North-Central part of Nigeria. He hails from Lavun local government of Niger State. His Nupe/English poems have featured in Kalahari Review — an African eccentric literary journal. He is also an artist and calligrapher with some works exhibited during some Book and Arts Festivals in cities like Kaduna, Minna and Abuja. He is an advocate for the infuse of mother tongue in contemporary literary works to preserve them from extinction. He likes learning Nupe proverbs to strengthen his vocabulary and broaden his scope of the language. Follow him on twitter @abuu_yaman

Aristea Papalexandrou was born in Hamburg in 1970. She has published six books of poetry: Dio onira prin (Two Dreams Ago, 2000), Allote allou (Once, Elsewhere, 2004), Odika ptina (Songbirds, 2008), Ypogeios (Underground, 2012), Mas propserna (It's Passing Us By, 2015) Nychterini Vivliothiki (Night Library, 2020). She has studied music and Medieval and Modern Greek Literature. She works as an editor. For her book It's Passing Us By, she had honored with the Academy of Athens Award "Petros Haris", in December 2017.

Archie Swanson's poetry was first published in 1973 in English Alive, an anthology of South African High School creative writing. Poems have regularly been published in the quarterly South African poetry magazines – Stanzas and New Contrast. They also appear in the Best New African Poetry Anthologies (2015 through 2020), Experimental Writing: Africa vs Latin America (2017), Experimental Writing: Africa vs Asia in 2018 (two poems in Japanese), Vol. 1 & 2 of Africa vs North America (2018; 2019) and Writing Robotics: Africa vs Asia Vol 2 (2020). Poems were translated by the Spanish poet López-Vega and published in the Spanish National Newspaper, El Mundo (2016) as well as the Bolivian newspaper Correo Del Sur (2016). In 2017 two poems were long listed for the Sol Plaatje Award and the poem flashback was shortlisted for the UK Bridport Prize. His poetry has also been anthologized in Absolute Africa! (2018) and Naturally Africa! (2020) curated by Patricia Schonstein. Nine poems were short listed for the 2018 and 2019 AVBOB Poetry Competition and 'my geurnica' was chosen as runner-up in the English category in 2019. His first collection of poems, the stretching of my sky, was published in 2018 and a second collection the shores of years, in 2019. He has been a regular guest poet at Off the Wall Poetry, the Cape Town Central Library Poetry Circle, the McGregor Poetry Festival and the Prince

Albert Lees Fees (2018 and 2019). Poems have appeared in the Poetry in McGregor Anthologies (2014 through 2020). The poem 'déjà vu' was the inspiration for a Grant McLachlan composition for clarinet, violin and piano performed in the Baxter Concert Hall in May 2019. In July 2020, two poems were translated into Spanish and published in the South American literary journal Libero America. In August 2020, the poem 'afourer' was selected for the Clemengold Poetry Writing. Archie Swanson serves on the Board of the SA Literary Journal. He is an avid surfer who lives in George. www.instagram.com/poetarchie

Introduction

Although I don't often write in my mother tongue as I wish to, I value every time I do so. It is important that we, especially Africans, take time to write, communicate in our mother tongues, that way we preserve them from extinction. With varied statistics showing 9 languages become extinct every year, that's about a language every 40 days, it is important that we do all we can to preserve these languages. One of the most important way to preserve a language is to create scholarship, both written and oral, in the language, that way future generations can always have somewhere to start in learning the language, to read, to converse and do business in it…and it will continue to be important.

Africa as the cradle of human civilizations, has over 2000 languages, not to talk of distinct dialects, or part languages, so it's important that language and social science practitioners in Africa do the best they can to preserve the languages. Language is the heartbeat of the culture of a people, and in language we pass off, or down relevant survival information. In language we collect and create a sense of identity. Imagine if the humans hadn't created any languages, we wouldn't be any better than other animals…because our forms of communication will be limited to instinctual grasp of things.

With all these theories in mind I decided to create an anthology of indigenous languages of Africa and East Europe. If you are wondering why East Europe; it is one of the regions of the world that still communicate in indigenous languages, as each country in East Europe kept to its identity and didn't take to the dominant languages like English, French, Spanish etc… I am not saying it's bad to write in these foreign languages but it's important to stay close to the language of birth. So I asked writers from these two regions to contribute, it could poems, essays, and short stories, to this groundbreaking anthology of African and East European languages. This book is the culmination of that effort

We have work from 36 contributors (including translators) in several languages including among others Russian, Croatian, Macedonian, Greek, Bulgarian, Romanian, Turkish, Idoma from Nigeria, Igbo from Nigeria, Shona from Zimbabwe, Bemba from Zambia, Tonga from Zambia, Shingazidja dialect of Shikomori language of The Comoros, Chewa from Malawi etc... from writers residing in among others, Russia, Ukraine, Belarus, Romania, Greece, Bulgaria, Slovakia, Croatia, Zimbabwe, North Macedonia, Macedonia, Turkey, Malawi, Zambia, Kenya,, Nigeria, and The Comoros, writing around Love.

Love Notes: Everything is Love takes the approach that everything that humans do they do out of love. It could be love between intimate lovers, love between humans and the creators, love between friends, love between enemies, anger, hurt, distrust, in politics, business, social spheres; the driving force behind everything we do is love. The anthology is broad as it covers just about every human activity on earth and oncoming intergalactic life. There is a certain depth you find around love issues that permeates the anthology pushing the anthology into ecstasy and transcendence.

Δραπέτισσα (Σταδίου)
Aristea Papalexandrou

μούσα πολύτροπον...

Την ξέρω αυτήν την άγνωστη
Από το φως που άπλωνε
το μαύρο φόρεμά της
Θά 'λεγα απ' την ανάποδη
κι εκείνη πως με ξέρει
Νιώθω σαν να με παρακολουθεί
απ' τον καιρό που ασθμαίνουσα
τριγύριζα στην πόλη
Κι άκουγα λες και από μακριά
στο αυτί μου την σιωπή της:
«Άλαλη αντίζηλος γλιστρά
με φόρα στην Σταδίου»
Άλαλη αντίζηλος εγώ
Κι ορθώνεται μπροστά μου
Ωραία η νεαρά σιωπή
Με ξέρει και την ξέρω
Εγώ κι εκείνη
άσαρκη
στο μαύρο μου φουστάνι
Σαν κάτι θέλει να μου πει
Με τρώει για να με τρέφει
Γλυκά εισχωρεί στο είναι μου
Την τρέφω και με τρέφει.

1

The Fugitive(1) (Stadiou St.)

Aristea Papalexandrou
Translation by Philip Ramp

muse ingenious…

I know this stranger
By the light spread by
her black dress
I should put it the other way round
it's she who knows me
I feel like she's been following me
since the time when gasping
I wandered about the city
And I heard as if from afar
her silence in my ear:
"Speechless rival slip
into Stadiou swiftly"
I the speechless rival
And it rises before me
Lovely this youthful silence
It knows me and I know it
I and her
fleshless
in my black dress
As if she wants to tell me something
Consuming me to feed me
Sweetly permeating my being
I feed her and she feeds me.

Ρέκβιεμ για τον νεκρό που ομόρφυνε

Aristea Papalexandrou

Πάνω στα ειπωμένα
θα ειπωθεί και αυτό
μιας ληξιπρόθεσμης πληγής
το πρακτικό.
Έφτασε η ώρα της απογραφής
έμψυχα κι άψυχα
της περασμένης μας κοινής
ζωής όλα
τα καταγράφω
Στα δάχτυλά μου σε κρατώ
σκυφτόν
Σε σφίγγω κι ευθύς
Νάρκισσο
σ' ελευθερώνω
Απ' το ρομάντζο μας
ούτε έναν στίχο δεν κρατώ
Έναν επίλογο σωστό
δεν έγραψα
και ούτε

Requiem For The Dead Man Who Grew More Beautiful

Aristea Papalexandrou
Translation by Philip Ramp

On top of what's been said
this too will be said
the proceedings
on an injury that fell due.
The time has come for stock-taking
animate and inanimate
I'm recording
all the past we shared
in common
I'm holding you in my fingers
bent over
I squeeze you and like that
Narcissus
I free you
I am not keeping a single verse
from our romance
didn't write
a proper epilogue
not even

Τα εξ αδιαιρέτου
(Εν Πηλίω στοιχειωμένα)
Aristea Papalexandrou

Δεν ήρθε για κανέναν κατοικήσιμο
αυτό το καλοκαίρι
Όσο για τη βδομάδα αυτήν
των συναντήσεων
ξέπλυνε συγκινήσεις
αδηφάγες
Φιδίσιος δρόμος
ζεματιστός
κατολισθαίνοντας προς άπειρον
σκοτωμένα σκυλιά στην
άσφαλτο
δύσκολη η σκέψη για νερό
δύσκολη η ανάσα
Κι όταν αντίκρισες
χλομός
τα πρώτα στοιχειωμένα
από καιρό ακατοίκητα
όλα σε φώναζαν
να ξεκλειδώσεις
Τη θάλασσα, τη θάλασσα
Ξεκλείδωσε τη θάλασσα
Διώροφα τριώροφα
άδεια στην ερημιά
Όμως η πόρτα πουθενά
και το κλειδί σπασμένο

Ab Indivisio
(Haunted on Pelion)
Aristea Papalexandrou
Translation by Philip Ramp

This summer did not turn out
to be inhabitable for anyone
As for this week
of meetings
it flushed away ravenous
emotions
Twisting road
scorching
sliding toward infinity
dogs smeared on the
asphalt
hard to think about water
hard to breathe
And when wan you come
face to face
with the first haunted dwellings
vacant for years
they all cry out to you
to unlock
The sea, the sea
Unlock the sea
Two-story three-story
empty in a wasteland
Door nowhere to be found
and the key broken

Ndo mwelewano.

Balddine Moussa

Shiyengo kashizaya Lulu
Hayi! ngo n-dungo nende nda?
Mi mwa hunu bayishe kariziniya hu-mwedja!
Mi tsi zini wa-zina?
Hwamba ngamzino ndrabo?
Karitso yelewana hudrwadji!
Ye mizino yi heya mindji!
Hwamba wo wahangu wa kidjeni?
Badi sitso rongowa kidjeni! Hwamba mwelewo ndo watsonga?
Ngo mzino, wumani ndo watsonga?

The understanding
Balddine Moussa
Translated by ABDOULATUF DJALALYA

The hate doesn't give birth of treasure.
But from where you drive me out?
I am from here even though we don't dance in the same hold.
Don't you dance? Don't I do the same?
You find my dance mistaken.
That we content ourselves to listen to each other elsewhere than in the dance.
There exist several varieties of dances.
You say mine is strange, from Africa?
So is the language we speak too!
You say that it's for understanding each other?
Does the dance do the opposite?

Ndo wadjuzi
Balddine Moussa

Wanu tsi wadjawu wo wadjuzi
Yesa pvanu wazi djuliya ho hidjazi.
Imani yidjaliya yilepvu hata yeze ntsuli.
Ngwa huyiwo ha aya zindji wo-wakazi.
Mdjumwawo kapvu nyuma wuwo yaletsa hanawo.
Ngu mwono anduyi ye wu-hozwa ne roho yahahe, bo...
Bahata shadjaya kundi mlima ngwambo hawutsoho?

The know-it-all

Balddine Moussa
Translated by ABDOULATUF DJALALYA

Not like the others the knowers.
Those are standing out of Hedjaz.
Their faith adorns the chin and the half-leg.
They guide the faithful by verse.
Not more wise than them but with beard that exceed theirs.
He counteracts them, that look of love placed on them.
Even the half glass thinks it exceeds the mountains.

KUPITA KWANJI KOTERE
Kuleza John Lembi

Ikulasa magombe amasaya athuyi
Ndi misozi yosowa nayo chiyembekezo
Mwayenda ulendo wanu wotsiliza kutisiyila chitozo
Kupita kwanji uku a Magufuli

Wagwawu ndi mzati kusiya tsindwi panthaka
Wapita mkoko wogona mudzi wasauka
Tilile bwanji ife inu a Magufuli munali mtengo waminga
Woingitsa onse achibwana pochitapo mtambasale

Imfa ndiwe wanjiru kutenga awo timatsamilapo
Kusiya ana achibwana olila ndi wawo omwe nkodzo
Mwanka kunkhadze uko kudagona achete
Kuli ziii, sikuveka mau ngati umo ichitila bwinja

Imfa yanu yaziziritsa nkhongono za ambiri kuno ku Africa
Kupita kwanu kwatikumbutsa a Bingu padzana
Muzu wolimba uja Mugabe popita ngati maloto
Akuyenda chotengezana Gadafe yathu mitima idasweka

Tulo tanji iti toiwala nato adzukulu
Bala mwasiya yathu mitima ikukhetsa mwazi waululu
Tidzakukumbukilani kosatha ndi misozi yosauma
Tingoti wanuwoo mzimu mumtendere osatha wuuse

WHY DID YOU SAY GOODBYE?
Translation by Kuleza John Lembi

Flowing down our cheeks
Are tears taking away our hopes
You are gone leaving us in a shameful environment
Why did you choose to go like that Magufuli

The supporting pole has fallen roof to suffer
The elder is gone leaving the village with nothing to offer
How shall we cry for you Magufuli, like thorny tree you were
None could childishly play games besides you

Death you are selfish, why taking the shoulder to lean on
Leaving for us the useless with their weakness
To the dead where no voices are heard you are gone
The voiceless land like an abandoned old house

Your death has left many speechless in Africa
You have reminded us of Bingu the fallen hero
The strongest root Mugabe, like a dream he is no more
Peoples shoulders as they carried Gadhafi our hearts were broken

What kind of sleep is this to forget grandchildren
The wound you have left in our hearts so painful
Our tears will never dry remembering you
May your humble soul rest in peace

Lucruri singure
Adrian Suciu

N-are cum să nu fie frumos orașul din care vii tu,
de pe o stradă între două uitări.

Acolo se aud nesfîrșite fabrici de umbră
împachetînd lucruri singure. Vorbim despre ele
cum am semăna nisip în pustiu. Noi,
cea mai împlinită văduvă și cel mai vesel orfan.
Vorbim tăcerilor în case fără drum,
cînd nu iese soarele și luna mai așteaptă.
Se-ntunecă cerul de vorbe și seacă albia sîngelui.

În război există supraviețuitori. În dragoste, nu.

Iar mîinile tale sînt așa de curate
că poți spăla apa cu ele.

Lonely things
Adrian Suciu
Translation by Nicoleta Crăete

You can't but come from a beautiful town,
from a street between two oblivions.

There one can hear endless shadow factories
packing lonely things. We talk about them
as if sowing sand in the desert. Us,
the most fulfilled widow and the merriest orphan.
We talk to silences in houses without path,
when the sun won't come out and the moon goes on waiting.
The sky is darkening with words and the blood riverbed is draining.

There are survivors in war. Not in love.

And your hands are so clean
that you can wash water with them.

Păpuşa de cîrpe
Adrian Suciu

La dragoste şi la moarte nu se pricepe nimeni. Dovadă fiind
că iluziile omului despre dragoste
sînt identice cu iluziile omului despre moarte.

Pieptănăm toată viaţa păpuşa de cîrpe şi aşteptăm să zică: mama!

Ce spui tu, înţelegi numai tu, în zilele tale bune. Sau nu.
Dar în urma iubirilor şi morţilor tale
rămîn pisici părăsite şi cărămizi care vor să fie ferestre.
Rămîne numai vocaţia ta de sufleur în cimitirul eroilor necunoscuţi.

Ia-ţi păpuşa de cîrpe afară, ascultă cerul şi spune-i: mama!

The rags doll

Adrian Suciu
Translation by Nicoleta Crăete

Nobody is good at love and death. Proof being that
man's illusions about love
are identical to man's illusions about death.

We have been combing the rags doll for a lifetime and we expect it to
say: mother!

What you say is to be understood by you alone, in your good days. Or
not.
But following your loves and your deaths
deserted cats and bricks remain who would long to be windows.
Only your prompter calling lasts within the cemetery of the unknown
heroes.

Bring your rags doll with you outside, just tell her: mother!

Cutremure și femei
Adrian Suciu

La incendii și inundații, iubesc femei orfane,
cu picioare de lemn și mânere potrivite. Ele
nu vor nimic. Doar la cutremurele mari vor ele.
Când umblă câini împingând cărămizi
și bărbați târând praf după ei. Le port la înmormântări,
miresele mele sinistrate, inundate, arzând. Înghesuit
între cutremure și femei, bolnav și singur,
cobor în lume pe un râu ca o panglică aniversară.

Earthquakes and women
Adrian Suciu
Translation by Nicoleta Crăete

In floods and in fires and I love orphan
wooden-legged suitably-handled women. They
don't want anything. Only at the great earthquakes do they want.
When dogs pushing bricks wander
and men dragging dust along. I carry them at funerals,
my refugee, flooded, burning brides. Crammed
between earthquakes and women, lonely and sick,
I come down a river in the world as if an anniversary bow.

SÖZÜNDEN DÖNMEZSİN, DEĞİL Mİ?
Seda Suna Uçakan

O,
kapıyı son kapatıştı...
        Gözüme bilerek soktun orospu çocuğu!
Tam tamına 45 dakika -aralıksız-
....
....
....
....
....
....
....
....
....
....
....
....
....
....
....
....
....
....
....
....
....
....
....
.

-AY'N'I HALDE DURDUM-
Kar yağdı sırtıma,
        Zaman zaman...

YOU KEEP YOUR WORD, RIGHT?
Translation by Seda Suna Uçakan

It
Was the last slammering the door,
               You thrust it under my eyes intentionally son
of a bitch!
45 minutes in total -non stop-
....
....
....
....
....
....
....
....
....
....
....
....
....
....
....
....
....
....
....
....
....
....
....
....

-I PETRIFIED JUST IN THE SAME POSITION-
It snowed on my back
               From time to time…

MAPANGE
fred Sunday Mukanaka

:asuma konse kalatambwa
nabwenge yaleeta ukuminawila amate
:o umowapita,nkupunika nge mbwa!
shiku bumo nkasuka nkakufumbate.
)obushiku, imfula ikaloboka
be-fube akeema mu mpili
ıkushangila, amakufi yakafopoka
kupanga icibili.
:eemba: *'Comba malaila,'* ngo unwene
:asekaseka nge cimbwi
apula nangu ikesule, nshakanwene
:asambamofye ntimbwi, ntimbwi.
ıngu kasuba
)obushiku takakabalike
ıbufuba
)wali mu mfiifi, tabwakaliike.
nweshi ne ntanda fikashima
mukolwe tabakalile
ıngu nibacula mucishima
nani nkatoba yonse, nkapwile.
ıbipa nge cipowe
sha abantu imisakalala
ıati ukalila oweee!
o nkakufyompa nge mitakalala.

AMOROUS PLOT
Translation by Alfred Sunday Mukanaka

Every gem is admired
Delicacies make me salivate
Whenever you pass, I follow like a dog
One day I shall grab you.
That day it shall rain
There will be mist in the hills
Knees shall be bruised, holding on to you tightly
In our struggle to make a kiln.
I will sing: '*Comba malaila**like a pissed off man
I will laugh (howl) like a hyena
Luapula river may flood, but I shall not drown
I will happily swim *ntimbwi, ntimbwi.***
Even the sun
That day will not shine
It shall be jealous
Nshima will not be eaten in the dark.
The moon and stars shall be off
Cockerels will not announce dawn
Not even frogs in their ponds
I shall crack the eggs and sip the yoke.
I'm as bad as famine
Which leaves people emaciated
Lo and behold, you will moan *oweee!*
When sucked like a watery pumpkin.
*folklore song
**onomatopoeia

kulansha
fred Sunday Mukanaka

o nakutemwa, umweo kuti nakusuninako
pundu, uwabusaka nge kolongo
ba katambala nga nshifyonenako
li iwe, ndi nkolooko
hakwata bulo
hakwata tulo.
ngu mbiipe nga masambi
ngu nyende uwainama nge citepo
li mulonge, nakutemwa nga lyambi
kutemwa nge pepo
ulo ya lubuto
ashila ukucila ulubuko!
lapa, pali mayo uwamfyele
umina, nkakushitila icandaluwa
alamekelamo nga nakaitebele
nweshi nangu nauwa
ala-enda mu lubuto lyonse.
nwine musunga talamba minwe
fine shobe shonse shikapwa
ngu ukutumane ngo usuminwe
ngu utalale nga pa mfwa
umina, tauli mpokeleshi
pokeleshi busenshi.

23

ourting

anslation by Alfred Sunday Mukanaka

e way I love you, we shall share my breath
rgin, as graceful as a crested crane
ere you kerchief, I wouldn't wipe nostrils
r you I'm a clock
o not have a bed
o not sleep.
ough I'm as ugly as sins
ough I walk stooped
a barbell fish, you're the worm
ove you like prayer
e source of light
ore sacred than incantations!
wear upon my mother
wedding dress I'll buy, say yes
ce *nakaitebele** in its cocoon, elegant
en without the moon
ght will always be there for you.
ave blind love for you
our acne shall disappear
ough in sombre silence
ough lulled like one bereaved
ou won't be token of gratitude, say yes
kenism is a bygone custom.
caterpillar-like worm which moves about in a
coon covered with twigs.

24

ıkambala
'fred Sunday Mukanaka

o nshilafwa, ndafwaya ukuyako ku Nakambala
ɔo bushiku, nshakalye ubwali, nga bwanshi?
ɛatemwa nga kapooli mu cifwani ca mbalala
ɛatema icisaali, nkabike panshi
ı cintelelwe, umwatalala kwati bushiku
ɟo pakulya, nkaicefye nomushinku.
ɛaya na Okapi iminwe ikacekwa
kuti abeene bekanjikata
ɛalya kumo nefiseekwa Nga filya mona aba ku
ıipata
lya imbeba kumo nomucila
ya tulya kalundwe, amabuula nemishila.
ıkambala, odi uko naisa
ıngu ubelame ku bu-Tonga
ıi uko, imfula yaisa
imwisusha milonga
ıisa, naleeta ubowa
ıisa, nkulange ifyo tusowa.
ıntale mfise Okapi muli basampala
ɟenda kupula enda nakape
ıi uko, Nakambala
ıisa, nangu ibala lisape
ɟhitiina, kocamofye umulilo
ɟela, impuku shalafuma ulubilo.

25

Nakambala*
Translation by Alfred Sunday Mukanaka

Before I die, my desire is to visit Nakambala
That day, I won't eat nshima, what for?
I'll be as fitful as a pig in a crops field
I'll cut cane and put down
In a shade as cool as night
My stature shrinking when eating.
I shall carry a knife, Okapi not fingers
To avoid being caught
There will be no peels
Like people of Chipata do
Eating mice with fur and tails
The way we value cassava leaves and tubers.
Nakambala, odi (hello) here I come
Even if camouflaged there in Tonga-land
Odi there, rains have come
Streams shall flood
I have come with mushrooms
I have come to show you how we hunt.
Let me hide Okapi in my shabby clothes
A beggar moves with a bowl
Odi there Nakambala
Field may be weedy, I have come
I won't fear, fire shall burn
And mice will scamper.

*Nakambala is in Mazabuka district, Southern Province of Zambia where most
Tonga people live. It's famous for being a sugarcane estate.
This amorous poem therefore, is dedicated to all Tonga women. I love you.*

Abanto Baminto, Naseki?
Bonface Isaboke Nyamweya

Nche bweka, ng'ikaransete aiga namayianda
Engi eekomena egekoba kiane gianse
Nyiate? Yaya!
Eekombuchera kare yane ase amaote ane

Nainyoire kegima oborabu bwabo bwogoukoria
Amariogi abo kagotimbochoka
Buna emerangwa yaigogete
Bakaumoka gocha ime, bakomongera igoro nainse

Bakaumamia chimesa
Ase tata na mama betukerete
Amo nainche.
Obokendu bwarenge gokang'ia ase ebaranda

Bakorigamora, bagasureka aang'e
Amaiso asongororogete gocha ase tore
"Uuuui!" mama agaaka egekuro
"Kira kiri! Inwe teri abanyangongo. Ebinyambi."

Obosio bwokoondokia bokang'usa ensemo
Abwo agekumba na koinda egesire…
Amanyinga agasiaroka korwa ase mama na tata
"Ebinyambi!" bagachengera. "Ebinyambi biatogokire!"
© *Bonface Isaboke Nyamweya*

27

My People, Why?

Translation by Bonface Isaboke Nyamweya

Lonely, I sit down here morosely
A fly licks my lower lip.
Crush it? I can't!
It taps my past into my sores

I sure recall their darkening lights
Their cracked voices bubbling
How doors swung open
They poured in, peeping up and down

Upturned the tables
Where papa and mama hid
And myself.
It was bitingly cold on the floor

Sweating, they drew near
Eyes elongated towards us
"*Uuuu*!" Mama screamed
"Shut up! You're not natives. Weeds."

A towering ugly face pulled me aside.
Then he slouched and swung an axe…
Blood spat on me from papa and mama
"Weeds!" they jubilated. "Weeds are off!"

СИНЏИР ОД ПЕСОК
Borche Panov

синџир од песок
до тебе плетев од брегот
и чекав
морето да го повлече синџирот мој

колку ли алки од месечини
за тебе исковав
во синџир од приливи и одливи

еден ден недосонет од ноќта
извлечи ми една алка
од синџирот на дишењето

и кога ќе подигнеш бран
повисок од ветрот
и ќе ме повлече силата
со која го создаде животот

еден миг само
биди алката
што ми недостасува љубов
и гледај како сè одново почнува...

CHAIN OF SAND

Borche Panov
Translation by Daniela Andonovska-Trajkovska

I was knitting a chain of sand
from the shore to you
and I was waiting
for the sea to pull my chain in

how many rings of moons
I have forged for you
in a chain of tides

one day as endless dream dreamt by the night,
pull out a ring for me
from the chain of breathing

and when you'll raise a wave
taller than the wind
and when I will be pulled in by the strength
with which you have created the life

be the ring
that I miss for at least a moment, my love
and see how everything begins again...

ЦРВЕНИ И БЕЛИ ЗРНЦА
Borche Panov

додека
тревожно жонглирав
со моите црвени крвни зрнца
жонглирајќи со бели крвни зрнца
дојде и ти
и додека траеше играта страсна
во која ги смешавме зрнцата
одеднаш
да внимавам ми рече ти
зашто ни едно зрнце не смееш
да загубиш
белите – за да живееш
црвените – за да ме љубиш

RED AND WHITE BLOOD CELLS

Borche Panov
Translation by Daniela Andonovska-Trajkovska

while
I was attentively juggling
with my red blood cells
you came along, as well
juggling with white blood cells
and while the game of passion was taking place
in which we have mixed all of our cells together
to be cautious you said to me
at once
because not a cell you are allowed
to lose
the white ones – you need to live
the red ones – you need to love me

ВЕЧЕН ДОЖД
Borche Panov

Стоиш помеѓу капките дожд
што лебдат околу тебе
како сите неизречени зборови мои
со кои те љубам
повеќе од љубовните пораки,
коишто тивко минуваат
низ сите жици и сателити
и светот го држат
како и јас тебе в прегратка нежна...
Те гледам низ капките дожд,
а секоја од нив -
секавање со секавање, сон со сон,
живот со живот спојуваат
и по лицето твое течат
и пак си толку убава
како и првиот пат, кога надвор од времето,
ме бакна со сето време на овој свет.
Заштитени од тишината на дождот,
меѓу капките стоиме двајцата ние
и љубовта ко силуета на ангел
оцртана под дождовната пајажина
и одеднаш од молњата ноќна осветлена
во еден град којшто траеше сал еден миг -
доволно да се сетиш
како на светлината од животот свој
со мислите ко со сенки
си играш на еден ѕид за кој и денес не знаеш
колку силно удираш со дланките,
кога со кошмар на усните се будиш
и никогаш не си сигурна
што ли се вистински се случило

среде тие секогаш поинакви секавања,
кога на рацете твои сум умирал...
И пак се продолжи,
кога една сенка си играше со телото мое
во таа летна ноќ,
кога и сонцето и месечината и небото
лебдеа со молскавицата в капките дожд,
додека те гледав и препознавав,
додека ме гледаше
и да те изустам чекаше, Љубов моја...

ETERNAL RAIN

Borche Panov
Translation by Daniela Andonovska-Trajkovska

You are standing alone among the rain drops
that hover around you
like all of my unspoken words
with which I love you
more than the love messages
that pass silently
through all the wires and satellites
and that hold the world
like I hold you in my arms of tenderness…

I see you through the rain drops,
and each of them is binding -
memory to memory, dream to dream,
life to life
and they are falling down your face
and you are so beautiful
as much as you were at the beginning, when outside the time,
you kissed me with the whole time in this world.

Protected by the silence of the rain,
among the drops, the two of us are standing,
and the love like the silhouette of an angel
drawn under the spider web of the rain,
and suddenly you become all lightened by the night lightning
in a town that lasted for a second –
yet enough for you to relive
how on the light of the life of yours
with your thoughts as being shadows

you are playing on a wall that you don't even know
not even today,
how hard you hit on it with your palms,
when you are waking up with a nightmare on your lips
and that you could never be certain what has really happened
in those constantly changing memories
when I have been dying on your arms…

And it continued,
when a shadow was playing with my body
in that summer night
when the Sun and the Moon and the Sky
were hovering in the rain drops along with the lightning,
while I was looking at you and while I was recognizing you,
while you were looking at me
and while you were waiting for me to pronounce you: My Love…

СО СЕТО ВРЕМЕ ТИ ЗБОРУВАМ

Borche Panov

Има мигови кога се оддалечувам од се`-
се до средината на разделбите
и животот што одминува -
доволно далеку,
кога по најдлабоката воздишка
ќе ми остане само еден здив
и се` уште чекам да се појавиш од непросторот,
па во себе те прашувам
може ли со еден збор да се повлече еден миг.
И, го замолив мигот да ми повлече еден час,
часот еден ден,
денот - ден од утре и задутре,
сите денови - сето време,
и дали можеш да го почувствуваш сето време
со кое ти зборувам,
додека стоиш безвремена -
со едната дланка во мене
процветана како најнежен цвет
на кактусот на мојата трпеливост-
со другата,
со шамиче полно со заминувања
за да живееш насекаде со моите далечини,
некаде каде што душите наши
се тешат
во нивната нераскинлива рамнотежа
и помиреност во само еден збор
со кое стануваме безвремени,
збор којшто со сета надеж на овој свет
го изговарам,
збор во кој да веруваш е исто што и да љубиш.

WITH THE WHOLE TIME I SPEAK TO YOU

Borche Panov
Translation by Daniela Andonovska-Trajkovska

There is a time when I grow distant from everything,
when after the deepest sigh
I expect you to show up from nowhere,
and I try
to pull out a moment with only one word,
to ask the moment to pull out an hour for me,
the hour – a day,
the day – a day from tomorrow and the day after tomorrow
all days – whole time,
and I wonder
will you ever feel the whole time
with which I am talking to you
while you are standing timeless –
with one of your palms blossoming
like the most tender flower
on the cactus of my patience –
and with a handkerchief full of goodbyes
in the other one,
so you could live everywhere with my distances,
some place where our souls
are comforting each other
in their unbreakable balance
and reconciliation in only one word,
with which we become timeless,
a word in which to believe
is the same as to love.

içe geliş (fısıltılarla)
Çağla Bölek

gece rüzgarları getiriyor
yazılmamış olan hikayeyi
yazılmamış olan hikayeyi
(yazılmamış olan hikaye için)

portakallar düşüyor, okyanuslar daralıyor, kalpler yok oluyor
zaman; öğle batımında düşer.

*gerçekliğin sonu geliyor -içeri

gece yarısı yaprakları düşüyor
kıyafetler yok oluyor
teller, udlar denize açılıyor
-kemikler; ay doğumunda erir-

çocukların uzuvları ilk düşendir
ilk düşen
düş
düş
d

*geçekliğin sonu geliyor -içeri

kuzu büyüyor
mükemmel canavar kuzu. muhteşem yaratık, çoğalıyor
-burada, zamanın yenilgisinde
nefes daralıyor, dans içine karışırken, gelişirken, dans içine karışırken;
kapsayıcı zarafet.

boğazlar sessizce çığlık atıyor, boşuna, dalmamak için büyülü uykuya

39

ki o yerde

bildikleri her şey benimdir
düşledikleri her şey benimdir
hissettikleri her şey benimdir -de

limitin yokluğunda

bırak (düş)

sonrası aradıkları her şeyi onlara vereceğim
ilkin ne varsa içeride
kaybettirip, bıraktırıp, memnun ettirdikten sonra.
serbest bırak, bırak, bırakılışı
tüm günahlarını.

*gerçekliğin sonu geliyor -içeri
(uyanıklığının ve rüyanın arasından)

düşler yazılmak isterler
düşler yaşamak isterler, düşler canlanacaklar
düşler kurgularını yiyecekler

geliyoruz, geliyoruz uyanıklığının ve rüyanın arasından
tatlı uykunun ve sabah yalanlarının arasından
tatlı terin ve gelgitlerin arasından
sen geliyorsun içten (senin içinden)

kutsal değerler yok oluyor her adımla ve erken ölümlerle
güvenli alan, güvenli ortam, güvenli zarafet yiyecek hepsini.
ruh
orgazmları
bulacak
hepinizi

dualitenin sonu geliyor -içeri
(uyanıklığının ve rüyanın arasından)

bırak (düş)
bırak (ak)
bırak (dondur)
bırak (kavra)
bırak (yakala)
bırak (yatıştır)
bırak(doyur)
bırak (ürper)
bırak (inan)
bırak (hayal et)
bırak (serbest)

coming in (all in whispers)
Çağla Bölek
Translation by Çağla Bölek

night winds bringing
the story hasn't been written.
the story hasn't been written
(for the story hasn't been written)

oranges falling, oceans sinking, hearts disappearing.
time; collapses at noon down.

*end of reality comin in -in.

midnight leaves, falling
human clothes, vanishing
strings citterns, sailing
-bones; melt at moon rise-

children's limbs are first to drop
first to drop
drop
drop
(p)

*end of reality   comin in -in

lamb is growing
the lamb, the perfect monster, magnificent creature; bulking
-here, in the reverse of time-
breath tightening as dance merging as emerging as dance

merging as embracing grace

throats are silently screaming in vain, to not to fall for magical sleep
where

everything they know is mine.
everything they dream is mine
everything they feel is mine -as well

here; (where) the limit is none

drop (fall)

and i will give them all they seek.
after make them loose, release, please all in -within
break
break
-breaking free from all sins.

*end of reality comin in -in
(between your wake and dream)

dreams want to be written
dreams want to live, dreams will come alive
dreams will eat your scheme

we are comin, we are comin between your reality and dream
between your sweet sleep and, mo/urning lies
between your sweet sweat and, tides
you are comin within (your within)

sacred values vanishing with every step and early deaths
safe place, safe space, safe grace will eat them all
soul
orgasms
will
find
you
all

*end of duality comin in -in
(between your wake and dream)

 (end of duality comin -in
between your wake...

drop (fall)
drop (flow)
drop (freeze)
drop (grasp)
drop (seize)
drop (appease)
drop (please)
drop (creep)
drop (believe)
drop (dream)
drop (release)

Rudzi rwako
Simbarashe Chirikure

Ichi chimanikidzo handi chedu toga,
Mumba muno takaomerwa pamwe nenyika yose.
Iyo nyika nepasi rose hukama imbada nguva dzino,
Amai vatsva musana mwana achitsvawo dumbu.
Taiti zvatanzi tigare pamusha,
Taiwana nguva yekurezvana,
Zvishuwo zvemwoyo tozadzisa.
Zvino zvowongogara uri kwindi,
Wati ndidiniko mudiwa?
Rwawaisindipa rukudzo hauchada narwo,
Yekugeza mvura hauchandipa,
Kana dzangu mbatya kugeza nekuchisa hauchaziva,
Nhasi wabuda rudzi rwako chairwo.
Nhamo yandionesa paumire chaipo.
Handini ndakaunza denda iri mumwe wangu.
Chishuwiro chekudzokera kumushando ndinacho chose,
Asi kune mitemo iri kutisunga.
Sekerera zvako mudiwa tifare,
Inguva chete iyi nhamo inodarika.

Lockdown conflict

Simbarashe Chirikure
Translated by Oscar Gwiriri

This Covid 19 pandemic is everywhere,
We're suffering; the nation is suffering too,
No country seems to have enough aid for another
It's a world disaster, quasi-nuclear war
I expected to have ample time
Between you and me during this lock down,
But you seem to be exhausted of me being around you
And you swing and sway in your bad moods every time,
But is it my faulty darling?
You have change big time and no longer care for me at all.
Now I can see your true colours, after all is it my fault darling?
It is my wish to cope up with the family needs unaided,
But what about the strict lock down rules and regulations?
Hold my hand and embrace me once again my dear darling
This lock down monster will be over soon, and I'll love you even more.

Ndizvo zviripo
Simbarashe Chirikure

Ndidzodzi dzatiwira vatete,
Hanzvadzi yenyu yatisiya,
Matizwa neakakusiirayi zamu,
Zvinodzipura mwoyo tete,
Zvakadaro hazvo imi motochema muri ikoko,
Iniwo ndichisvimha ndiri kuno,
Ko, tingagodiiko nhai chihera?
Mukandimbundira zvimwe ndingakuchekayi nerakagomara,
Mukandimbundira zvimwe mungandiitewo kafira mberi.
Tarirayi pano vanhu vagere setsanga,
Hongu setsanga pamuguri wemadaranganwa
Vazukuru venyu Matiridha naTobhiyasi,
Ndakatovati vagare ikoko, kuno vasauya,
Basa rotobatwa nesu tiri kuno,
Ndizvo zviripo tetewe,
Huwandu hukapfurikidza mwero pano,
Kunyangwe zvaitwa murudo,
Mweni wekuuya asina kukokwa uyu,
Wekuuya pasina gogogoyi uyu,
Iyeyu ari pakati pedu uyu,
Anobva amera zenze nokuita manyawi,
Hazvizivikanwi tete imi,
Dzimwe nguva angatiputikira tose sechimambaira,
Tikasara tangova murakatira pano.

Way it is
Simbarashe Chirikure
Translated by Oscar Gwiriri

Condolences dear aunt,
We have lost our dear brother
Through this nasty pandemic
What can we do, besides exercising social distance?
You mourn in isolation where you are
And let me do likewise, dear.
We are gathered,
But like distant like maize cob grains far apart.
I have already sent word to my faraway children,
Matilda and Tobias are not coming either,
We will do the burial arrangements on our own
There is nothing more we can do, my dear
If we all choose to gather for mourning
Transmission will be a time bomb
Which will perish all of us dear.

CINCIN YEKO
Abdurahman M. Abu-Yaman

Ke bayeko na,
acin ga cincin ndocizhi e so lo nakan zawangi o
bambe kpikpe zawangi

Wun ga a lo dan nakan o zo,
kanga zana nyangban wo e tsu ya na
wun a de lokaci na wun ga nakan we tsu gbanyi ke katazhiko na

Kami na cincin yiri nana ga de kafa to lokaci na
wun ci a nakan wo wan anigaga na
kanga ga etsanman nya zana wo e wa na
ga zhe ke shariangi na ya we yi o
kanga ga ezanda eyelo nya zana wo e wa na
a ce ko we tukpangi o
**(Written in Nupe language: spoken by the Nupe tribe in North
central part of Nigeria, mostly located around the River Niger
areas of Northern Nigeria)**

COLD LOVE
Translation by Abdurahman M. Abu-Yaman

Just like cold weather,
that's how some type of lobe sneaks into your body
without your notice

When it finally spreads inside your body
that's when the person your heart is dying for
will seize the time to lock your body like a prison

When this kind of of love gets the space and time
and traps your body like this,
that's when the laughter of your beloved
becomes like a tickle to you
that's when the catwalks of your beloved
begins to pinch you

ЕЛЕКТРОНСКА ЉУБОВ

Daniela Andonovska-Trajkovska

љубовта денес се продава во излозите на желбите
во Книгата со маски каде сите имаат селфи
со duck face на очајот
како поп-ап на меланхоличното секојдневие
во општеството во кое сè може да се купи
за само 299 денари и каде сè е на 50 посто попуст,
а само душата е вистински намалена

ELECTRONIC LOVE
Translation by Daniela Andonovska-Trajkovska

love is on sale in the shop windows of the desires
in the Book of Faces where everyone is taking a selfie
with the duck face of the despair
as pop-up of the melancholic everyday
in the society in which everything can be bought
for only 2.99 Euros and everything is on 50 percent discount,
but the soul is what's really reduced

НУЛТИ АГОЛ
Daniela Andonovska-Trajkovska

во очекување на полноќ
од градите го истиснуваме остриот агол

ти легнуваш врз мене
јас се раѓам во нулата

NULL ANGLE

Translation by Daniela Andonovska-Trajkovska

in the expectancy of the night
we pull out the acute angle of our chests

you are laying down on me
I am being born in the zero

КРВОТОК НА НОЌТА
Daniela Andonovska-Trajkovska

Крвните зрнца на твоето и моето време
дишат во спотнатите капки на нашите проѕирни тела
кои си разменуваат
едновалентни анјони и органски јони
во координатниот систем од молчеливи зборови
пред гласно да се распрснат во крвотокот на ноќта

CIRCULATING NIGHT
Translation by Daniela Andonovska-Trajkovska

The blood cells of yours and my time
breathe in the sweaty drops of our transparent bodies
that exchange anions and organic ions
in the coordinating system of silent words
before they burst loudly in the night that circulates in us

ИСТРКАЛАНА ИГРА
Daniela Andonovska-Trajkovska

играта помеѓу тебе и мене
ги пие врутоците на огнот
испружен меѓу две нерамнини
кој се тркала по трите точки на реченицата
во породилната болка на универзумот

ROLLEN GAME

Translation by Daniela Andonovska-Trajkovska

The game that we are playing together
drinks the fire springs
spread between two hills
and rolls on the three dots of the sentence
in the labour pain of the universe

КРВНИ ТОЧКИ
Daniela Andonovska-Trajkovska

по телото ми течат капки со заробено дишење
откако една ноќ создадовме
нови крвни точки на координатниот систем
од нашето сонувано време

BLOOD SPOTS

Translation by Daniela Andonovska-Trajkovska

drops full of captured breathing
are rolling down my body
after we have created
new blood points on the coordinating system
of our dreaming time

МОЛИТВА О ТЕБЕ
Eldar Akhadov

Прошу Тебя, Господи, дай тому самому человеку, который читает сейчас эти строки, всё, о чём он Тебя просит! Дай ему это полной мерой, как умеешь давать только Ты один! И пусть он будет счастлив во все его дни, а если невозможно такое, то хотя бы сколько-нибудь. Даруй ему крепкое здоровье и любовь ближних, понимание и сочувствие... Сделай так, чтобы душа его всегда светилась одной лишь любовью ко всему сущему, огради его от дурнословия, от обид и зависти, от войн и смертей, от боли физической и душевной, если же всё это неизбежно, - не покинь его и тогда, дай утешение. Спаси для него всё, что дорого ему на земле. Если же поздно просить об этом, - не лишай его памяти...Не знаю – верит ли в Тебя читающий сейчас эту молитву о нем, но даже если и не верит: помоги ему! Пусть он чувствует, что - не одинок, что нужен и любим... Милостивый и добрый мой Господь! Исполни это моё желание! Исполни его так, чтобы прежде, чем закроются глаза мои, я мог сказать:" Благодарю Тебя, Господи! Ты слышишь меня..."

PRAYER ABOUT YOU

Eldar Akhadov

Translation by Isa Akhadov

I beg You, My Lord, give the Man, who is reading these entries, all that s/he begs You for! Give it to him/her full measure, as only You can give this way! And let him/her be happy in all his/her days, and if not possible, at least to some extent. Oh Lord, give him/her good health and love of family and friends, understanding, and sympathy... Make his\her inner man to shine perennially with love to all existence. Shield him/her from swear-words, bitterness and grudging, wars and deaths, misery and mental anguish. If all this is destiny, do not leave him/her, give consolation. Save all that is precious to him/her on earth. Even if it is late to beg for it, do not deprive him/her of memory ... I am not aware if the worshipper reading this prayer is believer in You. But even if s/he is not: help him/her! Let him/her not feel alone but be needed and loved...   Oh My Lord, the most Merciful and Compassionate! Fulfill my wish! Fulfill it in a way that, before I close my eyes, I could say: "Bless You, my Lord! You hear my prayers"!

КРОМЕ ТЕБЯ...

Eldar Akhadov

Я порвал все твои фотографии.
Но это не помогло. Я помнил тебя.
Я уехал за тридевять земель и больше не возвращался.
Но это не помогло. Я помнил тебя.
Я встречался с другими, и меня любили.
Но это не помогло. Я помнил тебя.
Я напивался - вусмерть, как сапожник, как бич, как последняя
тварь.
Но это не помогло. Я помнил тебя.
Я женился, обзавелся детьми, стал домовитым.
Но это не помогло. Я помнил тебя.
Я старею. Всё выветривается из памяти.
Всё.
Кроме тебя.

EXCEPT YOU...

Eldar Akhadov

Translation by Sir Brian Henry Tomlinson

I tore all your photos.
But it did not help. I remembered you.
I went very far and never came back.
But it did not help I remembered you.
I met with others and was loved.
But it did not help. I remembered you.
I got drunk - like dead, like a shoemaker, like a tramp, like the last creature.
But it did not help. I remembered you.
I got married, had children, became home-grown.
But it did not help. I remembered you.
I'm getting old. Everything is eroding from memory.
Everything.
Except you.

XIV.

Elena BĂLĂȘANU

Marea preoteasă nu a tremurat
în fața femeii. Știa câteva descântece,
scria versuri și le lega cu sfori de mătase.
Femeia se știa pe ea, știa
din ce este făcută și nu a tremurat.
Șerpi, descântece, jocuri și bărbatul
în mijloc.

XIV.

Elena BĂLĂȘANU
Translation by Nicoleta CRĂETE

The great priestess did not tremble
in front of the woman. She knew some charms,
she would write verses and then tie them with silk strings.
The woman knew herself, she knew
what she was made of and she did not tremble.
Snakes, charms, games and the man
in between.

PRIMA ATINGERE E FĂRĂ LUPTĂ
Elena BĂLĂȘANU

unde se oprește dragostea
și unde începe lupta
femeia îmblânzită deschide
cele patru ferestre
și nu vorbește despre ea
știi și tu
e o femeie pierdută
a învățat să trăiască pe jumătate
ca multe alte femei înaintea ei

FIRST TOUCH IS UNOPPOSED

Elena BĂLĂȘANU
Translation by Nicoleta CRĂETE

where love ends
and struggle starts
the tamed woman opens
the four windows
won't speak about herself
you as well know
she's a lost woman
she's learned to halfway live
like countless women before

CUM SĂ ÎŢI SPUN TRECĂTORULE
Elena BĂLĂŞANU

te cunosc
stai deasupra la patru
adesea îţi plouă în casă
şi de necaz o snopeşti în bătaie

HOW SHOULD I TELL YOU PASSER-BY

Elena BĂLĂȘANU
Translation by Nicoleta CRĂETE

I know you
you live upstairs at four
rain frequently pours in your house
and out of spite you do beat her to death

ÎN FIECARE SEARĂ CECILIA ÎȘI FACE CUIB
Elena BĂLĂȘANU

își pune întâi pernele
una peste alta
jucăriile
cărțile
își lipește apoi
urechea
de pieptul meu

și pentru că nu știe
să numere bătăile
spune că inima
bate în așteptare
închide ochii
oftează profund
și adoarme

EVERY NIGHT CECILIA MAKES A NEST

Elena BĂLĂȘANU
Translation by Nicoleta CRĂETE

she begins by putting the pillows
one on top of another
the toys
the books
and then she sticks her ear
against my chest

and since she cannot
count the beats
she says the heart
beats waiting
shuts her eyes
heavily sighs
and falls asleep

Mitsitsi Ya Dazi
Joseph Daniel Sukali

Mitsitsi yachita dazi m'kumila kwa dzuwa
Paliwombo pan'ka natukula anga ali m'phukila
Nyonga zasimbwitikira kuchikhokhombe
Minyewa m'kumatewa kuli kutsinika ndi liwiro
Lamum'chenga ndi nthawi fumbi umabwira ndi iwe

Chilimwe chadutsa koma mphukila kulibe
Mitsitsi yogwamkumina idakatinyongabe mun'thakamu
Wefuwefu kupumila m'phanthi miphuphu ya nthawi yanga
Tsogolo la mawa lapanililidwa kunkhwapa ndi tsogolo la dzana
Kucha kulikonse ndi chiyambi cha md'ima
Nthunzi uliwonse tingathawire ndi kuwala kwa dzuwa

Mipando yonona ili mkuutsa zilombo mwa angelo
Liuma la olamula andale limaposa mfiti yaikazi
Mtera owathetsera mankhalu ndi imfa yokha
Ife ndi yani kuti tisakhumbire kuzula mitsitsi
Olo kukhale kuzikumbira manda bola kusiyana n'kufa tili moyo
Nthawi yakwana mphukila ziphuke
Ndipatse nkono nzanga tichotse mitsitsi yovunda

Bald Roots
Translation by Joseph Daniel Sukali

As the sun sinks, roots have turned bald
The fontanel keeps pursing like an infant sprouting
As the vital force gets bulldozed to its base
The muscles shrink with fatigue from the race
Racing against time is vanity

The rains are gone but there are still no sprouts
Very old roots still choke us in their exhaustion
My peers and I gasp in pain hopelessly
The future suffocates under the armpits of the past
Every sunrise is but new dawn of darkness
Every shade we run to is but scotching sun.

Positions of power turn angels into monsters
Politicians can be *coldhearted than the she witch*
Only with death do we do away with them
Who are we to not desire the uprooting of such roots?
Even if that means digging our own graves, it's better than being dead
alive
It's high time the bud sprout
Help me comrade in cutting off these rotten roots!

О ТЕБЕ
Ruslan Pivovarov

О тебе потаённые мысли мои,
И в тебе мои вечные муки,
Но сгорая в горниле безумной любви,
Я хочу целовать твои руки.

Я хочу в этих дивных глазах утопать,
Как глубокое море бездонных,
Прикасаясь к тебе, обо всём забывать
От блаженства объятий нескромных.

Видеть сны о тебе, но не жить в этих снах,
Не ловить безнадёжно виденье,
Но с любовью безбрежной нести на руках,
Наилучшее Бога творенье.

Руслан ПИВОВАРОВ г. Лида, Беларусъ

ABOUT YOU
Translation by Ruslan Pivovarov

My secret thoughts are only about you,
And only in you is my eternal torments,
But burning in the crucible of mad love,
I want to kiss your hands.

I want to drown in those wonderful eyes,
Bottomless, like the deep sea,
Forget about everything, touching you
To be blissful from immodest embraces.

To dream of you, but not to live in those dreams,
Don't catch a hopeless vision,
But to carry in your arms with boundless love,
The best creation of God.

Ruslan PIVOVAROV, Lida, Belarus

76

ПОРТРЕТ ЛЮБИМОЙ

Ruslan Pivovarov

Для Вас готов слагать сонеты
И оды в Вашу честь писать.
Я Вам хочу дарить рассветы
И в росах утренних купать.

Могу часами забываться
В раздумьях сладостных о Вас,
Как пред богиней преклоняться
Готов от света Ваших глаз.

На звёздный холст ночного неба,
Я нанести хочу портрет,
Который в мире создан не был…
Той женщины, что краше нет.

Руслан ПИВОВАРОВ г. Лида, Беларусь

PORTRAIT OF A BELOVED WOMAN

Translation by Ruslan Pivovarov

I am ready to compose sonnets for you
And write odes in your honor.
I want to give you dawns
And bathe in the morning dew.

I can forget myself for many hours
In sweet thoughts about you
Ready to bow down like a goddess
From the light of your wonderful eyes.

On the canvas of the night starry sky,
I want to draw a portrait,
Which has never been created yet ...
The most beautiful woman in the world.

Ruslan PIVOVAROV Lida, Belarus

ГУБЫ ЛЮБИМОЙ

Ruslan Pivovarov

Тот не тонул в блаженства море,
Кто не касался женских губ,
Кто у любви не был в фаворе,
Кто скуп на чувства, сердцем груб.

Не получал ценнее дара,
Кто поцелуем награждён.
Сей вкус изысканней нектара,
Я в том всецело убеждён.

Любимой губы, страстью вея,
Так соблазнительно нежны,
Они влекут, надеждой грея,
Слова при этом не нужны.

В них тайна чувственных желаний,
В них наслажденья дремлет стон,
Их шёпот – музыка признаний,
Их близость – сладкий, чудный сон.

Руслан ПИВОВАРОВ г. Лида, Беларусь

LIPS OF THE BELOVED
Translation by Ruslan Pivovarov

He did not drown in the sea of bliss.,
Who hasn't touched a woman's lips.
Who was not in favor with love,
Who is rough-hearted and stingy with feelings.

He never received a more valuable gift,
Who is rewarded with a kiss.
This taste is more refined than nectar,
I am absolutely convinced of this.

Lips of the beloved, winnow passion,
So seductively gentle.
They attract, warming with hope,
Words are superfluous here.

They are the secret of sensual desires,
A moan of pleasure slumbers in them,
Their whispers are the music of confessions,
Their closeness is a sweet, wonderful dream.

Ruslan PIVOVAROV Lida, Belarus

TIRNAK İÇİ – İÇKİLİ – SALYALI – BİR – ŞİİR
Göktürk Yaşar

"Şöyle başlayacağım:
-*Bir tavşan beni beylik tabancasıyla avladı...*"

...
Sonra belki yeniden adlandırabilirim sevgiyi.
Kuşkum yok ama anlatacaklarım kısıtlı.
Üstünkörü hayat, sol ceketimin cebinde,
Deliyor yüreğimi ve sancılarla yalnız başıma bırakıyor beni.

Kan kanı saklar ancak söz dili parçalar,
Işığın şiddeti ne kadar çok olursa kahrolur, yanar.
Pullarım yok, aslında yinelenmekten korkuyorum.
Kusmuklarım kesiklerimdir, keskilerim.
Sarhoşum, mutsuzum ve monarşiye direnmekten yanayım.

Dahası ölümle yaşlanıyorum, öç alıyorum.
Adi bir kapitalist gibi!
Renklere küsmüşlüğüm yok, kim demiş?
Sadece yarı pornografik – yarı tavşani renk arayışındayım.

İşlemek istiyorum kılcal damarlarına en küçük yanılgıyı,
Ne gelecek kaygısı bu bendeki güzelim ne de ilenç kusması.
Sevmek; realistlere göre beyinde bir urdu.
Âşıklar buna yaseminlerle yürümek derdi.
Nihilistlere göreyse bir hiçlikten öteye gidemezdi...
Fas'tan bir kent, bir arya, bir sevgili, bir şiir çıkardım.
Gettoları yıktım.
Peygamberleri katlettim yüreğim de.
Ve tanrıyı da... - *Unutmadım...* -

Şimdi:
Kelimeleri alın, hırpalayın, yakın!
Umarsız uğraşmadır zaten her şey gibi şiir de, bir şair için...

IN THE NAIL -DRUNK- SLOBBERY-A-POETRY

Göktürk Yaşar
Translation by SEDA SUNA UÇAKAN

"I 'll start as:
-A rabbit hunted me with its service revolver..."

...
I may name the love later.
No doubt but those I 'll tell are limited.
Slight life, in my left pocket,
Is drilling my heart and leaving me alone with aches.

Blood hides blood however say smashes langue,
It burns, downs the more the light is in intensity.
Not having scales, I am afraid of being repeated in truth.
My vomits are my cuts, my cutters.
I'm drunk, sad and go for resisting monarchy.

More I'm getting older with death, taking revenge.
Like a mean capitalist!
I'm not cross with colours, who says it?
Just looking for a half pornographic- colour. (**yarı tavşani**)

I wish to manipulate the least delusion to your capillaries,
This is neither the fear of the future my darling, nor curse vomiting.
Love was a tumor in the brain to realists.
Lovers called it walking with jasmines.
As for nihilists, it wasn't more than nothing...
I got a city, an aria, a lover, a poem from Morocco.
Wrecked ghettos.

Murdered the prophets in my heart.
And -I did not forget...- god either.

Now;
Take the words, burn!
Poetry is already a helpless struggle for a poet like everything else.

Nhamo yemaricho

Oscar Gwiriri

E-e! Nhai imi changamire!
Ndicho chii chamuri kundiitira ichi?
Chokwadi here murume mukuru,
Kuti nganganga hembe muchiuno,
Pamusha pazere vanhukadzi kudai?
Kuitawo here nhai ikoko?
Munoda kuti vaite sei?
Ko, kuita maricho kuti shamai here?
Heya, ndizvo zvamange muchida,
Kuti mucheukwe-cheukwe?
Vachionei patumasahwa twetumbabvu twenyu tunosemesa?
Sei musina nyadzi imi sekunge dzinotengeswa?
Haiwawo, chitorai badza renyu mubve pano izvozvi.
Tumbabvu tunenge twembwa ine gwembe!

Piece work hurdles
Translation by Oscar Gwiriri

Hey you, man!
What the hell do you think you're doing,
What's your nerve, mature as you are
Immorally exposing your pseudo six pack
Amidst my wife and vulnerable daughters?
Can't you do this piece work fully dressed?
So, it was intentional of you,
To attract their attention as you have done,
With your skeleton nauseating ribs?
Pick your damn hoe and leave my yard.

Kumusha
Oscar Gwiriri

Pane rukuvhute ndipo pako chaipo,
Kumusha kwako ndiko kumusha,
Hakunazve musha unokunda wako musha.
Dai ndadzoka zvangu kumusha
Sezvo ndiri waikoko kumusha,
Zvisinei kuti handicharangarira
Kuti kumusha kwaive kwakadini.
Dai zvaigoneka hazvo,
Amai vandibvumirawo
Kudzoka mudumbu mavo.

Home
Translation by Oscar Gwiriri

Home sweet home!
Home is best.
There is no place like home,
I wish to go back home,
I really belong home,
Even though I don't remember
What it was really like.
I just wish mom to accept me
Back into her womb.

IPAKI
Austin Kaluba

Ninshi amenso nayafuma namumutwe kwati kabundi
Insele shalefumine mukanwa
Umwashindailwe ichisalu
Shasusishe imipashi yonse
Makumba, Mulenga wa Mpanga, Chishimba...
Shimwalule mukalamba alikoma namatwi kunsele
Lelo insele tashalefuma fye mukanwa mweka
Pantu shalefuma napamenso.
Insele shamumushingo ukuchila neshitukana makunkutu
Uulesamba iminwe yamilopa muchishima chachintubwingi.
Balimulalika ku mutwe wa mfumu iyafwa, iyakosa ngelibwe
Abena mushi abaishibe uko ali, balilosha nankwe mumitima yabo
nokumupepelako ukuti afwe bwangu
Afume namuchalo umo abatuntulu bashindika abafwa.
Moneni!
Imfumu shalufyengo shichili naifwe
Nomba shilefwala amasuti
Nokwingila munga'anda yamafunde.
Tuleshitatakwila ilyo shiletekesha ama meeting
Ukwabula nokumfwa akafungo kakubola.

Ipaki
Translation by Austin Kaluba

His eyes popped out of his head
Like a frightened bush baby
His muffled voice hissed insults at all deities
Makumba, Mulenga wa mpanga, Chishimba
The chief embalmer heard his curses
Not only from his stuffed mouth
But from his grotesque face.
As hideous as Hades' keeper.
The curses were more insulting than that of an amputated thief
Washing his bloodied hands in the communal well.
Finally, they lay him beside the lifeless chief, dead as a rock
The villagers who knew of his plight silently pitied him
Praying for his quick exit to the other world.
Away from a place where the living accompany dead royals.
Alas!
The dead chiefs are here with us
They were suits and debate in parliament
We hail them at rallies and meetings
and stand their stench

#Ipaki, *singular for amapaki (plural) were chief escorts (living human beings) who were buried alive to accompany dead chiefs.*

КОГАТО КОЛЕНИЧА
Мария Филипова-Хаджи

Когато коленича днес пред хляба
или пред ненаписан стих,
прости ми, Боже, трябва да призная,
че първият ми залък е горчив
и първата ми мисъл все засяда
на гърлото. И вместо да изричам
молитвено-хвалебствени слова,
една сълза отвътре ме задавя
и ме заставя да мълча.
... Ала утеха в мене натежава,
че утре този свят ще бъде нов,
защото плачът е пречистване божие,
а всяка сълза е любов.

WHEN I KNEELING
Maria Filipova-Hadji
Translation by Rumyana Todorova

When I kneel today in front of the bread
or in front of an unwritten verse,
forgive me, God, I have to admit
that my first morsel is bitter
and my first thought always goes stuck
on the throat. And instead of saying
prayer and praise words,
a tear from the inside strangles me
and makes me keep quiet.
... But the consolation in me is heavy,
that tomorrow this world will be new,
because crying is God's purification,
and every tear is love.

НЕСТИНАРСКА
Мария Филипова-Хаджи

Озъбени сенки
       прибулят мисълта ми.
Между прозореца и улицата
              просветлява.
Това е знак:
       в мене се разгаря
пак оня огън луд
и върху пламъците му игриви
ще затанцува песента ми жива.
Тупа-тапа, тупа-тапа –
Нестинарски ритъм
       сърцето ми отмерва.
И думите се сипят
       като въглени –
те цял живот
       отвътре ме изгаряха,
ала сега са
       моите икони.

NESTINAR*

Maria Filipova-Hadji
Translation by Rumyana Todorova

Toothy shadows
veiling my thought.
Between the window and the street
enlightens.
This is a sign:
it kindles me
that fire crazy again
and on its flames playful
will dance my song alive.
Toupa-tapa, toupa-tapa -
Nestinar rhythm
measuring my heart.
And the words drop in
like wooden coals,
which all my lives
burned me inside,
and now they are
my icons.

Ancient dance into the embers with icon in hands and nude feets.

КЪМ БЪЛГАРИЯ

Мария Филипова-Хаджи

Ще танцувам на пръсти,
да не смущавам музиката,
с която ме докосваш.
Ще танцувам полека,
за да чувам дъха ти —
от него се стопявам
и ставам на капка…
Не си ли жадна, Майчице?

TO BULGARIA

Maria Filipova-Hadji
Translation by Rumyana Todorova

I will dance on my toes,
not to disturb the music,
which you touch me with.
I will dance slowly,
to hear your breath -
I melt from it
and I become a drop...
Aren't you thirsty, Mother?

Срамниче
Мария Филипова-Хаджи

Била съм, може би десетина годишна. Отивахме с мама на лозето. По пътя тя току откъсне някоя билка и ми разказва за нея. Веднъж откъсна едно бяло цвете, с плосък цвят, образуван от много малки цветчета едно до друго, с дълга дръжка. В средата малките цветчета образуваха една черна точка, приличаща на петно, голямо колкото нокътят на палец. Мама ми разказа:

- Това цвете се нарича Срамниче. Някога целият му цвят е бил черен, но с годините срамът на хората намалява и виж как е останало само едно малко петно. А си спомням като малка, че само по края имаше една бяла ивица и цялото беше черно. Тогава не вярвах на приказките на баба ти, че цветето се е променило заради срама на хората, но сега се уверих.

Да си призная, аз също не повярвах на мамините приказки и колкото пъти съм се сещала за това през годините, все си мислех, че е било нейният пореден урок за възпитание. Но запомних цветето.

Това лято в Средна гора видях край вилата си същото цвете. Едва го познах. Огледах го отвсякъде, да се уверя, че е то. Същото си беше. Само дето на някои цветове имаше една едва забележима черна точица, а на повечето - никаква. Беше си чисто бяло. Думите на мама излязоха верни - нямат срам вече хората. И природата "документира" това на свой език.

Само че аз си измислих друга приказка: още малко и чернилото от душите на хората ще изчезне съвсем и ще се пречисти светът - ще стане чист и бял.

На вас коя от двете приказки ви харесва?

A Bashful Flower

Maria Filipova-Hadji
Translation by Azam Obidov

That time, I was about ten years old. Together with my mother I went to the vineyard. As we walked down, she kept bending over a grass, then over the other one, and the next, and as she touched a grass, she began to tell me about its medicinal properties. One day my mother tore a white flower with a flat inflorescence, formed of several tiny blossoms on a long stem. There was a tiny black dot similar to a spot, no bigger than the nail of the little finger, right in the center of the flower.

"This flower is called a bashful, shy flower", my mother said. "Once, all its petals were black, but over the years people have become less and less conscientious; there have been less shame and shyness, and more shamelessness, that's why only one spot is seen here. I remember that in my childhood, the flower had wavy white stripe only at the edges and the whole flower was black. I did not believe the stories of your grandmother that people have changed over the years, and they are increasingly losing not only shyness, but conscience as well. But now I'm convinced of this."

I confess that I did not believe my mother' stories either, and throughout my life, when I remembered our tour of the vineyards, I thought that it was her next life lesson. However, I still remember that flower.

This summer, in the middle of the mountains, not far from the villa, I saw a flower of my childhood. I could hardly recognize it. I looked at it thoroughly to make sure that it really was the right one. I saw that it has changed over the years, only a few small petals with black spots remained. Now it was almost white. So my mother's words proved to be true: people have no conscience. And nature "documented" it as it is. And then I came up with a new tale. I thought that there is a little more time and the blackness of human being's soul will disappear forever, along with the flower. And the world will be cleansed of dirt and becomes lighter, cleaner and more beautiful.

So, tell me please, what kind of tales do you like most?

Gombeza
Marita Banda

Gombeza ilo mukuona na nika pa nthambo, ndane
Lene lila liswesi na babulaula bati bii mu mphepete
makora ghene, ndane
Ndipo, lu saba kuomila cha

Mungaleka kulisezga apo nkhulibika namweneco, ku
chipinda
Kwambula ku nimanyiska

Gombeza lane nkhudikha para kwiza ka mphepo
Para nadikha mbwenu kati fuu... Makora ghene

Gombeza ili nanga inunkhe folo, ndane
Panji mukunuska matuzi, ngane
Nanga ni nyelemo viskuli vya nchunga za msuzi uswesi,
ndane
Asi lu chapiwa? Ilo lili pa nthambo likuomila makora
ghene

Ningafika patali yayi kwambula gombeza lane liswesi
Na babulaula bati bii mu mphepete makora ghene

Nyengo zinyanke lusebeza nge ni nkhata
Nkhuthwikilapo maji pa kufuma ku dambo
Ndipo, pa kufuma ku thengele nkhutwikilapo nkhuni
La dazilo nkhayeghelamo mboholi wuwo makora ghene

Nkhumanya banyake pa imwe banyithu
Kumasinda uku muka nenanga kuti 'Haki ukazuzi bati!'
Kweni mboholi muli kulya
Nati nane lino nkhubetcha

100

Gombeza ndilo lane!
Ukazuzi nawo, ngwane!
Ntheura, mukhale waka chete!

Gombeza likunilela na mweneco,
Likunisunga
Ndipo ndiwemi nkhanira

Chinyakeso... Nkhumanya pali banyake pano
Nyifwa yindanunkhe imwe muli yamba kale
Kuibendelela gombeza ili
Kuti muzalitole para nyifwa yanifikila
Agho maghanoghano mulekeletu
Chifukwa ili gombeza nkhunjira nalo m'dindi

Olo nyifwa yinitole,
Ndine wonozgeka kale
Imwe mbwenu chitanda muza mubika mu gombeza ili
Mungasuzgikanga kuti mu gule linyake chara

Muzamusebezeska lene lili gombeza lane
Liswesi na babulaula bati bii mu mphepete makora
ghene

My Blanket
Marita Banda
Translation by Simon A. J. Banda

See the blanket, drying on the clothes line,
Yes, the red one with decorative black butterflies on the
edges. It's mine
Guess what, it won't be long before it dries

Please do not move it from where I put it in the bedroom
Without my knowledge

When there is a cool breeze, my blanket feels nicely
cosy,
Wrapping it around my body I snuggle in it

Even when it reeks thick stink of raw tobacco, I own it
Sometimes you can smell pee, I know, well, that's mine
too
I don't mind farting in it after a hearty meal of red beans,
in rich creamy sauce I own it. It gets washed, right?
Look! It's on the clothes line getting dry

I cannot get too far
Without my red blanket with the decorative black
butterflies on the edges

Sometimes, it serves as a cushion for my head when I
carry heavy loads
Like pots of water from the dambo
Or firewood from the forests
Just the other day, I wrapped sweet potatoes in it from
the fields

I know, some among you were making silly comments
like,
'How disgusting!'
But later you came to eat, and even enjoyed my sweet
potatoes
Well now's my turn to boast;
See, the blanket is mine;
The filthiness too, is mine,
That being the case I say, suck it up, dude!

The blanket is good for me;
Nurturing and taking care of me

Oh..., and another thing; I'm aware of your speculative
scheming; gossip mongering
Even before the smell of death nears you are already
deliberating about who'll get my precious blanket when I
get bumped off the planet
Stop that nonsense right now! I intend to be interred with
my blanket

Should death come for me today, oh baby, I am ready; I
mean bring it on!
Here's the plan: You will wrap my remains in my red
blanket, yes the one with the decorative black butterflies
on the edges.
To hell with your fancy caskets or new blankets
My precious red blanket with the decorative black
butterflies on the edges
Will suffice

ZANGA!

Marita Banda

Zuba la njila,
Ndipo mwezi nao waca
Nchakwenerera kuti wize ku nyumba
Nchakwenerera kuti ubeluke ku zi nchito za ku minda
Manyi wafikira ku mphara ya madoda
Welako! Nyengo yamara

Zanga mu khonde,
zanga ticezge ta'bili,
Mu nyengo gha'mise muno, zanga tisekepo
Tibekane mu maso
Tilabiske mukati gha maso gha citemwa,
Ndipo titaike mwenemumo

Zanga
Tiphalilane viweme-viweme, vyaunenesko vya ku mtima
Nkhukhumba ku manya maghanoghano ghako ghaweme kwa ine
Zanga uni phalile m'khutu mazgu ghakunowa
Mazgu ghakuteremuka pa lulimi nge ni uci,
-Kuti skererere
Mazgu ghakunyong'omera pa kumira pa singo, -Kuti ske-e!

Zanga pa duze, fika pafupi, zanga uni guze pafupi
Zanga niku tofye-tofye, niku fyofyonthe
Nikukhumbatile, nikudikhe,
Nifwase nawe nacitemwa camafuta kuti fye-e! Nananananaaa...!

Zanga mwana wa 'nyamuNyirenda
Mu khonde muno, muk'pita ka mphepo ka weme nkhanira

Zanga tipembe moto pamoza, tipembe moto wacitemwa

104

Ughu moto tilik' buska tabili-bili
Nchakwenerera kuti tipembe pamoza
Para waleka kubuka, panji wakana kunyeka
Citemwa ici, nge ni sima, ci bisikenge

Nati Zanga mwakufulumira, ufike pano mwalubiro. Wendiske ka!
Maji gha ku geza gha thumenge, cakulya naco nanozga kale
Fungo la dende la bakoma 'nyaMugezenge
Ndipo ba tinkha, Cifukwa
Afumu babo ba welako waka ku zengelo

Zanga
Tiphalilane viweme-viweme, vyaunenesko vya ku mtima
Nkhukhumba ku manya maghanoghano ghako ghaweme kwa ine
Zanga uni phalile m'khutu mazgu ghakunowa
Mazgu ghakuteremuka pa lulimi nge ni uci,
-Kuti skererere
Mazgu ghakunyong'omera pa kumira pa singo, -Kuti ske-e!

Zanga pa duze, fika pafupi, zanga uni guze pafupi
Zanga niku tofye-tofye, niku fyofyonthe
Nikukhumbatile, nikudikhe,
Nifwase nawe nacitemwa camafuta kuti fye-e! Nananananaaa…!

ZANGA!

COME!

Marita Banda
Translation by Simon A. J. Banda

The sun has descended
And the moon is high and bright
It is time you come home
You ought to leave the work fields
Perhaps you have stopped at the mpara?
It's time to get home. It is getting late.

Come relax in the veranda with me
Let's enjoy each others' company in the evening hours
Come we laugh out together
Let's look into each others' eyes
Let us gaze deep into the eyes of love
Let's just about lose ourselves in there.

Come,
We share our deep, honest and heartfelt affections
I want to know what beautiful reflections you have towards me
Come, whisper softly sweet words of love into my ears
Words so sweet they slide off the tongue like warm honey
Going drip-drip-drip...
Words so mellow, you just wanna imbibe them gracefully down the
throat

Oh, come real close now, draw ever so near, come, pull me to you
Come, I fondle and caress you, giving you a real nice rub down
Come, I kiss you, I hold you, I wrap you in my arms
I enfold and serenade you in the warm embrace of passionate love

Come, dear son of Ms. Nyirenda. Come join me the veranda
There's a nice, cool breeze blowin' in here

Come we light up the fire together, we enkindle the fire of love
Remember how we started this fire, just the two of us
It's essential that we keep it going
Should it stop glowing, or for any reason the embers quench
Like improperly tended sima, this love will be raw

Say, get here quick, I mean, a toute-vitesse-now! Hurry up already.
Your bath water is starting to cool, your dinner too is all ready
Ms. Mgezenge is getting all riled up over the savoury aroma from my
kitchen
And, she's just about hating on me right now
All this because, her husband came home from hunting without a kill

Oh, come real close now, draw ever so near, come and pull me to you
Come, let me fondle and caress you, giving you a real nice rub down
Come, I kiss you, I hold you, I wrap you in my arms
I enfold and serenade you in the warm embrace of passionate love
COME!

vis răsturnat
Nicoleta Crăete

iubirea e un eşafod pe care dormim
iar somnul nostru are ferestre cu vedere spre păsări

nu-ţi face leagăn din părul femeii îndoite cu apă
o pasăre şi-a făcut cuib în el
ca să moară

o vei planta a doua zi
şi vei şti
că nu ştii nimic din ce ştii
când cu mâinile oarbe pe trupuri citeşti

nu mai rămâne decât să legi copacii cu faţa în jos
să se oglindească pământul în ei când te cheamă
cu nume strain

overturned dream
Translation by Nicoleta Crăete

love is a scaffold where we sleep
whereas our sleep has a sight towards birds

don't make yourself a cradle from a watered woman's hair
a bird has built a nest in it
so it could die

you are to plant it the next day
and you will know
that you know nothing that you know
while reading on the bodies with your blinded hands

all you are left with is to tie the trees face down
so that the earth should mirror them when calling you
with a strange name

poem luminat
Nicoleta Crăete

frica s-a așezat la baza lumii să se odihnească un pic
deasupra niște furnici îi spărgeau semințe în cap
una două
șapte nouă

dar uite cum din urechea dreaptă răsări o religie
cu picioare prelungi
o adorau și adoratorii de mijloc
o adorau și adoratorii de stânga
că până și cei adorați o adorau
și ar fi fost prea multă armonie în lume
de n-ar fi fost

dar iată cum în urechea stângă furia creștea din stări limitrofe
războaie șuvoaie
le adorau și adoratorii de dreapta
și până și cei adorați le adorau

tu doar să-mi ții lumânarea să scriu

enlightened poem
Translation by Nicoleta Crăete

fear has sat down at the basis of the world to take a rest
above its head some ants were smashing seeds
one two
seven nine

but here is how from the right ear a religion has risen
bearing long legs
the middle worshippers would worship her
the left worshippers would worship her as well
even the worshipped ones would also worship her
and too much concord would have been there in the world
hadn't it been

but there is how from the left ear rage was growing up from final
moods floods
wars
the right worshippers would worship them
even the worshipped ones would also worship them

you just hold me the candle so that I could write

cine e acela ce umblă
Nicoleta Crăete

oamenii au uitat să respire
fragmente de gol
zac orânduite de-a valma
pe casele lor

vremea e să se audă orchestra
pândeşte cărnii hrana lor
umbră pământului

dar intră în alunecarea din umbră
cad păsări cad păsări
cu morminte în cioc
şi-ntrebarea

cine e acela ce umblă
fără haine şi nume
cine e acela ce umblă

who is that wandering one

Translation by Nicoleta Crǎete

people have forgotten to breathe
fragments of void
rest helter-skelter ordained
on houses of them

time for the bandstand to ring
of flesh lieth in wait their feed
shadowing earth

but come into the shadowy glide
birds falling birds falling
with tombs in their beaks
and the query

who is that wandering one
no raiment or name
who is that wandering one

ПРОСТОР НА ЉУБОВТА
Vesna Mundishevska-Veljanovska

Во време на
мегаломански аспирации,
наспроти тешкото врзување
крај со крај,
избравме да живееме
во две соби.
Често велиме – Тие се
нашиот мал рај.

Овде и ѕидовите
ја споделуваат
нашата самотност,
а тишината маѓепсува
со својата лечебност.

Воздухот издишува
опојна сензуалност,
а подовите испаруваат
под сеприсутната вљубеност.

Овде нашата дуалност
благословено катарзира
во тројност.

Во новооткриеното
суштествување
новата животворност
возвишува возљубеност.

Во спокојот на љубовта
просторот на двете соби

нараснува до беспросторност.

Љубовта
во нашиот рајски остров
е секвенца од времето
овековечена
во безвременост.

SPACE OF LOVE
Translation by Vesna Mundishevska-Veljanovska

In a time of
megalomaniac aspirations,
versus the heavy tying
end to end,
we chose to live
in two rooms.
We often say - They are
our little paradise.

Here even the walls
share
our loneliness,
and the silence enchants
with its healing calmness.

The air exhales
intoxicating sensuality,
and the floors evaporate
under the ubiquitous infatuation.

Here our duality
blissfully lives its catharsis

into trinity.

In the newly discovered
essence of the reality
our new vitality
exalts affection.

In the peacefulness of the love,
both rooms's space
grows to spacelessness.

Love
in our paradise island
is a sequence of the time
eternalized
in timelessness.

НА ВРВОТ НА ВУЛКАНОТ
Vesna Mundishevska-Veljanovska

Стоиме гушнати
во врелата тепсија на денот.
Сонцето пече, земјата вреска
а ти сенката си ја бараш
меѓу врелиот метал
на пожолтената трева.
Бараш вода,
водата по тебе тече.
Завиткани во лава
си ги стегаме рацете
и место вода
си ги подаваме срцата.

AT THE TOP OF THE VOLCANO
Translation by Vesna Mundishevska-Veljanovska

We stand hugged
in the hot casserole of the day.
The sun is shining, the earth is screaming
and you are looking for your shadow
among the hot metal
of the yellowed grass.
You are looking for water,
the water flows on you.
Wrapped in lava
we squeeze our hands
and instead of water
we give to each other our hearts.

реПРОДУКЦИЈА
Vesna Mundishevska-Veljanovska

Како камче сме
фрлено во водата
на растопените снегови
од пирамидата на поколенијата.

Како стог концентрични кругови
се лизгаме по мегникот
на мултипликацијата
на вековите –
круг во круг,
еден до друг,
еден по друг,
во еден друг,
подруг
простор
кој ни го плакне смогот
од бреговите на желудникот
со свежината
на заборавеното уживање
во мигот.

Во крошната од дрвото
од островот на дворот
вкоренето во грбот
на желката на безвремето,
празниот простор на човекот-сенка
нараснува како меур сапуница
кој навлегува во срцевината
на нечија туѓа граница
за да назре во внатрешноста на паралелноста
или да се распрсне во бесмисленоста.

Пак некои камчиња ми ги брануваат
водените пространства
под вулканот во душата.

А можеби сега,
токму сега,
во повторливоста
на некоја линеарна бесконечност,
баба ми со машата
го расчепкува мангалот на вселените.

И можеби сега,
токму сега,
во некоја паралелна идност,
и моите внуци
го приготвуваат слаткото од дунки
што го правам по рецепт од мајка ми,
која го запишала од мајка ѝ,
додека си ги рендам мислите
со вкус на еден сладок недостиг
кој лебди како кристална аура
околу иконата на спомените.

rePRODUCTION

Translation by Vesna Mundishevska-Veljanovska

We are like a pebble
thrown into the water
from the melted snows
from the pyramid of the generations.

Like a stack of concentric circles
we slide on the boundary stone
of the multiplications
of the centuries -
circle to circle,
next to each other,
one after another,
in one other,
differentiated other
space
that washes away the smog
from the shores of the stomach
with the freshness
of the forgotten enjoyment
of the moment.

In the tree crown
from the island of the yard
rooted in the back
of the turtle of timelessness,
the empty space of the shadow man
grows like a soap bubble
that enters the marrow
on someone else's border
to peek inside the parallellity
or to burst into meaninglessness.

Once again some pebbles wave
the water's surface
under the volcano of the soul.

And maybe now,
right now,
in the recurrence
of some linear infinity,
my grandmother with the iron tong
kindles the brazier of Space.

And maybe now,
right now,
in some parallel future,
my grandchildren at the same time
prepare the quince jam
that I make following my mother's recipe,
which she's got from her mother,
while I grate my thoughts
with a nostalgic taste of a sweet bliss
that floats on the air like a crystal aura
around the icon of the memories.

Ihotu
Ehoche Edache Elijah

Ihotu yo leche
Ihotu moyi ko leche
Ihotu kw'eyi ko'leche
Ihotu miu oogwonu ko'leche

Ihotu miu kusa ko ochi onyokpa
Ihotu kwogba dudu
Ihotu le gba lewa duuma
Ihotu agaa choota n'

Ihotu ka wa
Ihotu geyi bio gicho
Ihotu get mine chigbihi
Odadu no get bi

Ihotu yo ipoyi
Ihotu yo ipo ooyi
Ihotu w'ondu
Ondu wi'hotu

Love

Ehoche Edache Elijah

Love made man
Love endured man
Love replaced man
Love took man's fall

Love nailed at the cross
Love paid it all
Love paid for all
Love you can't ignore

Love says come
Love will take you up
Love will restore
That which was lost

Love in the blood
Flows from the Son
Love is God
God is Love

İncir Ağacı

Eşref Ozan / Ozan BAYGIN

hiçbir şey aslında hiçbir şey
ve sadece delilik
onarılmaz kırılmış çok kere
zeytin dalı kadar kutsal değil
olsa olsa incir ağacından
bir parça senin gözünde

The Fig Tree
Eşref Ozan BAYGIN
Translation by Sıla Ellie KUTU

Nothing is actually nothing and only craziness
Been broken too many times, cannot be fixed.
Its not as sacred as an olive branch
In your eyes, at most it can be a piece from a fig tree

Piçin Yılı
Eşref Ozan / Ozan BAYGIN

sabah sıfır altı : kırk dokuz boşul fırtına
bir bütünlük içermeksizin kaotik ve tektir

I.

Çanların usulca çaldığı
isli bir düş yolculuğunda
burnumda ıslak orman kokusuyla
dudaklarımın çatlayan kabuklarını dolduran nem
getiriyor hüznümüze mâtem.

unutmak zordur aynı kokuyu
çeyrek asırdır taşıdığım burnumda
içilen şeytanın göz yaşlarıdır
hayat dediğin sanrıdır
yüktür ana rahminden bu yana
ağır ve büyüktür
acısı cin kuyusunda gizli ağu
dolaşır damarlarımda.

Demle karışmış
baygın gözlerimden fışkıran sarmaşıklar,
önümde beliren tarantulalar
dallarıma kökümden tırmanırlar
hissedilen hep aynıdır hatırladığım
dört duvar arasında,
burnumda ıslak orman kokusuyla üstelik.

Çatlayan dudaklarımın kabuklarını dolduran nem
ilişir gözüme

127

belirir mâtem,
buğusuyla sırrını unutmuş mat ayna
usulca karşımda durur.

Sarmaşıkların diplerinden tutunmuş kükreten otu
duysa, aslanı yerinden sıçratır
Chemtrail bulutlarına neden olur
boğulur zaman
derinden bir uğultu duyulur
gözlerimi gözlerimden alamam.

Burnumda ıslak orman kokusu
her ağacın dibinde mantarlar var
yeni bir başlangıcın habercisidir
tırmanan karıncalar
omurga kemiğimden saç uçlarıma kadar
yarış yaparlar
bırakırlar larvalarını saç diplerime.
onarırım
aynanın kırık yerlerini.

II.
Sanrıyla-gerçeklik arasında, yakınken gerçeğe daha
o ilk inen sözün etkisiyle daldım uykuya ve
sonrasında mağaramı örümcekler korudu

bekledim tokadımı
sesinden sır vermeyen plasentalı
ebesiz peygamberler eşliğinde.

sol kulağımı kemiren yarasa yavruları,
sol kulağımın uğuldayan yanı ve
fısıltıların yükselen desibeli ilahi bir psikozdur.

III.
Gizemli uzuvlardan fışkıran alkaloitlerin etkisiyle
dalgaların saatte binbeşyüz kilometre hızla sahillere yayıldığı
bir hışımla kopan tufan,

balkonda brandanın renk değiştirdiğine şahit olan serserinin
düşünce gücüyle bulutlarda oturma isteği ve
binaların saygı duruşunda beklemeye başlaması,

devrilmeye ramak kala
kahkaha atan şairlerin ilenç uğultusu,

tutkusu olmayan sahte gülüşlerin düştüğü sonsuz boşluk ve
paralel evrene başlayan uzun yolculuk,

parklarda ve ıssız bankların üstünde terleyerek
titreyerek çenesi kilitlenmiş halde zaman kavramını eriten gömüt,

mum üstünde kanat çırpan kelebek, "Tesadüf"te bong ruleti
dostluğun en kutsal mertemesinde bayılıp
sabahın altı buçuğunda da tekrar
fokurtulara kulak veren deneyim tutkunları,

özgürce yaşamak için deliliğini savunan ve
özgürce yaşamak için deliliğini gizlemeye mahkum olan
yüce nesil.

Buz üstünde çırpınan son geyik
karadelikten baş göstermiş son solucan
damla damla eriyen son biçimsiz buz
Huxley'in kutsal adası ve giz
son dumanı çok sert çekmeliyiz
başka türlü nasıl bilebiliriz bu kutsal gerçeği ?

Yürüyün çocuklar
göğün rahmine gidelim
bilge Einstein'ın dileği budur
kudurtur yıldızların gülümseyişi...

Year of the Bastard
Eşref Ozan BAYGIN
Translation by Çağla Bölek

its o-six in the morning: forty-nine voiding storms
without any integrity, this is chaotic and only!

1.

Where the bell chimes silently
in a sooty vision trip
with wet forest scent
the moisture filling the gaps of my chapped lips
brings sorrow to our lament

it's hard to forget the same scent
carried for quatre-century by my nose
what is drunk is the tear of the devil
life is a delusion
a burden since the womb
heavy and grand
a poison where its pain hidden in a jinni well
wanders in my veins.

Mixed with spirits
ivies squirting from my fainted eyes,
tarantulas appearing in front of me
climb my branches from my root

what is felt is the same remembrance
between four walls,
moreover, with the wet forest scent on my nose.

The moisture filling the gaps of my chapped lips
catches my sight
lament manifests,
the dull mirror that has forgotten its mystery with steam
stands in front of me silently.

If the roaring weed clinging from the ivies' root
senses, it causes the lion to jump
calls out the clouds of Chemtrail
suffocates time
a hollow howl is heard

i cannot take my eyes off of my eyes.

Wet forest scent on my nose
mushrooms are under every tree
heraldists of a new genesis
the climbing ants
from my spine to the ends of my hair
compete
leaving their larva on the root of my hair.
i mend
the broken pieces of the mirror.

II.

Between the reality-the delusion, within reach of reality more
i fell asleep beguiled with the first word of revelation and
spiders protected my cave

i waited for my slap
accompanied by tight-lipped placental prophets
without midwives.

the baby bats gnawing my left ear,
the howling edge of my left ear and
the rising decibel of whispers is a divine psychosis.

III.

With the impact of alkaloids squirting from mystical limbs
The waves spreading on beaches as fast as one thousand five hundred
km per hour
here the great flood in rage,

the punk on the balcony who witnessed the awning changed its color
wishing to sit on clouds with mental power and
the awaiting of the buildings in homage,

the cursed humming of laughter of poets
on the edge of tumbling down,

the eternal void fallen by fake smiles without passion and
the beginning of a long journey to the parallel universe,

the tomb
sweating and shimmering its jaw-locked
in the parks and on deserted benches melting the concept of time,

mum üstünde kanat çırpan kelebek, "Tesadüf" 'te bong ruleti
the devotees of experience, adoring the holiest level of friendship
and again, at six-thirty in the morning
paying attention to the sound of bubbling,

the holy generation
defending their madness to live free and,
doomed to hide their madness to live free.

The last deer flopping on ice
the last worm arising from the black-hole
the last shapeless melting ice
the holy island of Huxley and mystery
we must inhale strong, the last smoke
otherwise, how to realize the holy truth?
March children
together to the womb of the sky
great Einstein's wish is this
smiling of stars maddens...

КРАЈОТ НА ТАЈНАТА
Zvonko Taneski

Вљубеник сум во македонскиот фолклор,
таму се чека - дур до гроба.

Јас ќе те чекам 100 години
и секој ден ќе биде јуни
и ти ќе внимаваш
другите да заспијат
пред нас
за да ми раскажеш
за своите синови, а јас тебе
       за ќерките
и за двете персиски мачки
со големи влакнести опашки

Ќе те чекам 100 години,
ама не повеќе.

END OF THE SECRET
Translation by Zvonko Taneski

I am Macedonian folklore lover
Over there one awaits – even to the grave.

I will wait for you 100 years
And each day shall be June
And you shall watch out
The others to fall asleep
Ahead of us
So that you can tell me
About your own sons, and me to you about my daughters
And about the two Persian cats with big furry tails

I will wait for you 100 years,
But not any longer than that.

МОКРА
Zvonko Taneski

На душекот целата мокра
лежи сонуваната жена

убиена
од будилникот

SHE'S WET
Translation by Zvonko Taneski

Entirely wet on the mattress
Lies the dreamed woman

Murdered
By the alarm clock

ЉУБОВ ПО ПИЈАНА НОЌ
Zvonko Taneski

Рано ќе си ги миеме забите
и долго ќе стоиме пред огледалото со пена в уста
ќе ја вкусуваме сопствената засраменост

Рано само ќе ме прашаш каде си го ставила саатот
а јас ќе те замолам
да го вклучиш радиото, спикерот на утринските вести
ќе нè поинформира за илјадниците студенти
кои си замнале дома за празникот
и тактички ќе помолчи за нашата последна ноќ во модерниот
                              интернат

Рано ќе се чувствуваме
многу напуштени и ќе излеземе
надвор на бучавите улици
буричкајќи по џебовите
при барањето на изгубеното време
и по важечкиот патнички билет

ветрот ќе дувне со празни раце
како невработен поштар
и радосно ќе ја одвее
згужваната картичка со набрзина запишаната непотребна адреса
па ќе биде толку непријатно
да се разделам од тебе
и да се потпрам
на студениот прозорец
во автобусот
и да молчам

ама сега зборуваме многу
низ грло ни поминуваат секакви признанија
подеднакво лесно како чашките,
па зборовите совршено
ќе ни се преплетат
и ќе одлетаме некаде нагоре
без да почувствуваме
дека оттаму го создаваме новиот човек

Making love after drunken night
Translation by Zvonko Taneski

We'll be washing our teeth early on
And we'll be standing long before the mirror with foam in our mouth
We'll taste our own embarrassment

You will merely ask me early on where you have put your watch
And I'll ask you
To turn on the radio, speaker of the morning news
That will inform us about the thousands of students
That had left home for the holiday
And she'll tactically say nothing about our last night in the modern
boarding school

Early on we'll feel
Very abandoned and we'll come outside
At the noisy streets
Searching through our pockets
While we seek out the lost time
And the valid passenger ticket

The wind will blew empty – handed
As unemployed postman
And joyfully will blow away
Crinkled card with hastily written unnecessary address
And so it will be so uncomfortable
To split apart with you
And to rely on
The cold window
In the bus
And to keep silent

Nonetheless we talk a lot now
All sorts of confessions are passing through our throat
Just as easy as drinking cups,
So that our words can be perfectly
Mixed up
And we'll fly somewhere up
With no sense that
Hence we're creating the new man

НЕЖНОСТИ БЕЗ ГАРАНТЕН ЛИСТ

Zvonko Taneski

Со оние кои за луѓето
создаваат убавина,
луѓето обично се однесуваат грдо.
...
Секоја револуција ги јаде своите деца, ама најпрвин
добро ќе ги накрми.
...
Според векот на автомобилот корозира и бракот.
...
Кој има среќа во картите,
ништо нема да изгуби
барем при разведувањето.
...
Со ширењето на феминизмот
и музите се приклонуваат повеќе кон авторките отколку
кон авторите.
...
Често пати ќе се договориме
за тоа што ќе биде утре,
а потоа нема да се договориме
за тоа што било вчера.
...
Во моментите на слабост
ќе кажеме:
„Ќе те изедам од љубов" –
и веднаш си закачуваме на врат кривично дело.

Јазот сé повеќе се продлабочува.
Нежностите се продаваат

без гарантен лист.

Tendernesses WITHOUT WARRANTY SHEET
Translation by Zvonko Taneski

To those that for the people
Create beauty,
People usually behave badly.
...

Each and every revolution eats its children, but firstly
It will well – fed them.
...

At the same time as the automobile, the marriage corrodes as well.
...

Whoever has luck at cards,
Will lose nothing
Well at least while divorcing.
...

With the spread of feminism
Even the muses incline more to the authoress than
        To the authors.
...

Very often we agree
About what will be tomorrow,
And then we disagree
About what it was yesterday.
...

In moments of weakness
We'll say:
"I'll eat you out of love" –
And we immediately lay a criminal act at our door.

The gap is growing.
Tendernesses are being sold
Without any warranty sheet.

САКАВ ДА ПИШУВАМ
Zvonko Taneski

Сакав да пишувам песна за тебе –
да те соблечам од сите метафори, метонимии и епитети,
да бидеш гола вистина,
официјална и прифатена од надлежните
како цврст доказ во самоодбрана
Сакав да пишувам порака до тебе
да те опишам како слегуваш кон мене со погледот прибран
без да се свртиш наоколу,
колку за проверка – да не те следи некој нескротлив и непримерен
Сакав да пишувам и-мејл до тебе
да потонам во твојата виртуелна нежност
и да самувам салноќ пред мониторот вклучен –
да не ми изгорат очите од мракот –
пред да те видат на јаве по подолго време
Сакав да пишувам писмо до тебе
да те наградам со милост –
да ја имаш како резерва или вишок,
кога подзаборавав да се насмевнеш за поздрав
Сакав да пишувам, ама веќе се премислив.
Така продолжувам и понатаму да сакам.

I WANTED TO WRITE
Translation by Zvonko Taneski

I wanted to write you a poem –
to strip you of all the metaphors, metonyms and epithets,
so that you be the naked truth,
official and recognized by the authorities
as a conclusive proof in self-defence
I wanted to write you a message
to describe you descending towards me
with a collected look,
without looking round
in case you're being followed by anyone
untamable or indecent
I wanted to write you an e-mail,
to arise in your virtual tenderness,
and spend the entire night lonesome in front of a running monitor –
so that my eyes don't burn out in the dark –
before they get to see you in person
after a longer while
I wanted to write you a letter,
to reward you with mercy
so that you have it in reserve or in surplus
whenever you forget to smile
when greeting
I wanted to write but I've changed the plan.
So I further continue to want.

Oge
Obinna Chilekezi

Ihe ndi nkpa nke nkwu
Ma anyi amagi tutu ofuo
Oge, ola edo nke oma
Anyi nile were oge haa otu
Ma anyi anagi eweya out oha
N'aka nwatakiri, oge adigi agwugwu
Ma na aka okenye, oge anagi ezuezu
Maka nkea, were kwa oge me ihe mara nma
I we be kwa akwa na oge na dighi anya
Maka oge nke I tupuru n'ohia

Time
Translation by Obinna Chilekezi

So precious to loss
We don't appreciate it so
Time, what a valuable gem
We all have equal time
But differently place values on time
For in the hands of the young, time's limitless
But the elderly, time's not enough
So use your time for the good
So that you don't cry in the future
For the time you had wasted in life.

die pad na Middelplaas
Archie Swanson

by Le Roux Stasie
draai die grondpad af na Middelplaas
volstuise wei in groen lusern lande
kronkelende leibeurt fonkel verby
vloedbesproeing weerkaats gebleikte lig
hoofsomer van 'n uitgestrekte jeug

ek kuier by my ouma en oupa
hul huisie langs die pad
koel voorstoep
gang tot appelkoos in agterplaas
sproet-gevlekte amber vrugte

maar nou is dit 'n ander somer
ek plaas my ma se as
langs haar ouers
en haar sister
en haar broer

die wereld lyk onveranderd
laatmiddag skaduwees
strek verby die watervoor

the road to Middelplaas
Translation by Archie Swanson

at Le Roux Station
the dirt road leads to Middelplaas
ostriches graze in green lucerne fields
winding water-turn sparkles past
flood irrigation reflects bleached light
broad summer of an endless youth

I visit my grandma and grandpa
their little house next to the road
cool front porch
passage to backyard apricots
freckled amber fruit

but this is another summer
I place the ashes of my mother
next to her parents
and her sister
and her brother

the world seems unchanged
late-afternoon shadows

Zvarwaireva kumukadzi uyu
Translation by Tendai Rinos Mwanaka

ZIta rake ndiEve, zita rakan'ora.
Anoritakura zita iri kunge angobva kurinhonga-
Mumativi enzira isina kufambwa nomurume uyu.
Mukadzi uyu imhomhi chaiyo, murume uyu imhomhikadzi.
Mukadzi uyu anosarudza murume uyu, nokuda kwake, Adamu-
Muiti wezvakashata, dzambiringwa munyemba, goritoto kushata.

Mukadzi uyu anodisa kugukuchira zvinhu.
Mukadzi ane mivara, uye inomuka-
Pose paanogumbatirana nomurume.
Kuti amuchengetedze mukati, mune izvi, rimwe zuva-
Izwi rake rinoyambukira nomumahwindo,
Rinoshandura nzira kuva huchi.

Kuti adzungaidze vapambi,
Ndozvaanonzwa apo anotsvoda murume uyu-
Kunge zvikwangari zvakasunama zvomunzira, kunge kurongapatsva.
Anoramba achitarisa Pandiri rewanano yavo,
Zvakakwana here zvakachengetedzwa, zvinokwana here kusvika-
Kuzambuko iro raakapisa kare, ndezvemariiko?

Mukadzi uyu aifunga kuti anogona kukunda hondo yemhomhikadzi iyi.
Nhingiti dzawora, asi nyenyedzi dzichiramba dzichimupa mhoswa asina
zvaaizvara.
Asi maEpuru akaoora akaramba achidonha mumaoka ake aigachira
zvose.
Haana kugona kuchengeta mashoma zvawo!
Akageza micheka yokuvatisa nemasodzi yake.
Achitarisa rudo rwake rwuchifa nokubhowekana.
Achirara mukushata kwekuswotwa kwekunhuwa kwemaguza ake.

152

Musiyano waiva pakati pokuvhima zvokudya uye kuvhima-
Mukunakidzwa nako, zvakafana nechidimbu chimwe chisipo
chechingwa chetsvutugadzike.
Kusatendera kwakakamurwa, kutendera kwepakati,hapasisina
zvichamurwadzazwe.
Mukadzi uyu anodisisa kuudza murume uyu kuti zvaakanyatsoda
mibvuri yake chete.

Achiri pazero remakore okupikata mazamu ake achiri madiki akamira-
Kunge twumwari twudiki twunehasha twuchirikutsvaga daidzo
yezvokwadi.
Anoona tarisiro irimumaziso emukoma wake mutswa.
Apo mukadzi uyu anokakata hana yake- kururama, nokutendeseka
kwakanyanyisa-
Kwouyo anoziva mukadzi wake.
kwomunhu anoda kupa zvose zvinodiwa nomukadzi wake.

Nzendo dzakareba pamusoro pemazamu ake zvinomurangaridza
nezvekufema.
Apo mukadzi uyu anenge achivhurira vharidziro yemvura yomurume
uyu.
Kubowa kwakasviba kwemabhanan'ana emwedzi wagunyana.
Nechemberi gorero vose vanosvika kumwedzi,
Uye vanotombogarapo pamusoro pemwedzi uyu.

What it meant to her
Tendai Rinos Mwanaka

Her name is Eve, a folly of a name
She carries it as if she has just found it
On the sides of the roads he never walked
She is a wolf, he is a werewolf
She chooses him, for him: Adam
The wicked, the misfit, the imperfect

She likes holding things in.
She has these colours and they wake
When she nestles with a man,
To hold him in, in that way, someday
Her voice slips through the open windows
Turns the streets into honey

To fool invaders,
Is how it felt when she kissed him?
Like out of order streets signs, rearrangement
She kept checking the pantry of their marriage,
Has enough been stowed away, is there enough to last
The bridges she has burned down, at what cost?

She thought she would really be able to take on the slaughtering
werewolf,
Rotting seeds, but the stars made her feel guilty when she couldn't
Only rotting apples kept falling into her welcoming hands,
She couldn't keep a few
She washed bed sheets with her tears
She watched her love dying from boredom,
Sleeping in the sour boredom smelling blankets

The difference between hunting for food and hunting

For the fun of it, is one sandwich less for breakfast
Half doubt, half believe, nothing will hurt her anymore
She really wants to tell him she only loved his shadows

She is still at the age where she bears her new breasts
Like pert little deities seeking rightful homage
She can see the look in her new boyfriend's eyes
As she pulls out his heart- the pure, terrible trust
Of someone who knows her
Someone who wants to give her what she wants

The voyage across her breasts reminds her to breath
As she turns on his faucet
The dark roar of a September storm!
Later that year they reached the moon
And they even landed on it.

Mudazvakawanda
Translation by Tendai Rinos Mwanaka

Waiva tsvarakadenga pachiso-
Asi ndaisafanira kukusarudza.
Nokuti kuvaka musha newe kwaive,
Kwakafanana nemaungira esimba egungwa.
Ini ndirikangarava kadiki kachishambira,
Pamusoro pemaungira aya. Uye iwe-
Zvawaigonesesa kundirunzira.
Nokundiputsira munyanza yako iyi.

Hana yangu yaiva rwiyo rwomunakamwa.
Ichipaparika paparika,
Ichinyuta mumazwi ayo.
Kuedzesera kushambira pamusoro penyanza iyi!
Kuti iwe undinzwewo.
Ndichingoramba ndichishevedzera nokuzhamba,
Kuti rushusho runodzvokora kubva-
Mauri, zvarunongoita nguva dzose!

Iwe zvako maziso ako achikandwa pese pese.
Iwe uchiti urikutsvaga zvimwe zvakawanda zvokuita,
Kunge rujeko rwezuva mangwanani.
Rwuri pese pese, kwesekwese,
Munguva imwecheteyo!

Asi ini ndichikuda zvokutopatsanura gungwa.
Kuti ndisaeredzwe naro, kunyangwe zvazvo befu rimwe-
Rinodziya, raindizorodza mumarwadzo, kusangorifema!

Paiva nokubwazhangukira mukati mangu-
Mandakachechedza mwoyo wangu kuvhurira,
Marwadzo okushivira rudo rwako.

156

Asi kunge munongedzo wokubuda mubishibishi rokurwadziswa-Goronga iri ririmumwoyo mangu richavharika munguva yakakodzerana.

multi-tasking
Tendai Rinos Mwanaka

You were so pretty to look at
But I shouldn't have picked you
Because being with you was
like waves in a big, ugly ocean
and I was a little boat ploughing
the waves and all you seemed
able to do was to lure me
off-balance

My heart was an accapella solo
still bubbling on
drowning in words
trying to surface
to get you to listen to me
i kept screaming, screaming
that difficulty looked out of you
the way it did.

Whilst your eyes wandered off
you called it multi-tasking
like the morning's example
that's all over,
everywhere
all at once

And I still loved you
like blowing up a float.
so I could not fly though
one breathe warm,
could have set me free.

There was a necessary tearing
where I scissored my heart open
on the painful side of your affections

But like guide out of hurt's
labyrinth.
the rift will seal in time

Vanodanana zvisina hanya.
Translation by Tendai Rinos Mwanaka

kugegedza kunobwinyabwinya kunge doro rehwisiki.
kubva mugirazi richangodirwa.
kugegedza kwakananga kuzuva.
tinokungurukirana pasi muvhu.
kugegedza kunge nyika-
isati yaenda kumawere.
shiri dzenziyo, kubuda kwezuva,
Kuvhumuka, kupunzikirana, kuita murwi umwe,
vevanodanana zvisina hanya, vasingatyi.
kugegedza kurikusvatukasvatuka kubva mune muti-
nomuti, mudenga rakachena.
muviri wake unotsemura wangu.
tinorariramo mukati make,
mukudanana kunouya nenzira dzakawandisisa.
kugegedza kwematombo kubva uko kuchienda uko.
kugegedza kwerwiyo rwemhepo rusinakurongeka.
kudambura zvidimbu zvemusungo yendangariro.

careless lovers
Tendai Rinos Mwanaka

Laughter spills like whiskey
From a shot glass
Laughing straight into the sun
We rolled onto the ground
Laughing like the world
Hadn't gone to shit
Song birds, sunrise
Delirious, we fell, a heap of
Careless lovers, invincible
Laughter bouncing from tree to
Tree, in an open sky
Her body split mine
So we lie in copula.
Lovemaking coming in many
Forms: a chime rocks to and from
Tinkling a random wind song
Breaking the memory fragments.

Hwezvero idzi
Translation by Tendai Rinos Mwanaka

Mudzimai uyu anokubata zvakare-
Kubatwa kuriko chete chiringiso chako.
Unofamba kupinda muzvinyoronyoro, uchitya zvikuru-
Kudonhera mune rimwe gomba rakadzama risina mvura-
Mukatikati, kupinda muhwanga,
Ukamugwejura nokumudonhedza.
Uchitya kumuganyabvura-
Zvine ukasha, uchiramba wakabatirira mundangariro,
Dzokuva kwako panguva iyoyi.

Muchingosasana zvenyu munguvashoma dzamambakwedza.
Muchibatirira patambo dzakanyorovera.
Muchiedza kusvikira iyo n'ain'ai kutaima-
Kwejecha rokumahombekombe omumwe nomumwe wenyu.
Vanodanana vaviri ava, vanezviso zvakavhenekwa nomwenje
wemwedzi.
Munotarisana, munonzvanzvadzirana nemaoko,
Munorasikira mumasango ekunaka kwenyama dzenyu.
Kutovana matama enyu, omumwe nomumwe.
Kupfekedza mumwe nomumwe-
nezvipfeko zvokudananisa kwenyu.

Rudo mafashafasha uye,
Zvakawandisisa zvokuita narwo.
Mose munodana umwe noumwe, zvinoratidza-
Kubva mukupa zvose uye kudisisisa.
Dzimwe nguva murunyararo, munezvatinosara nazvo,
Hakusi kudiwa, asi-
Kuti isu tadisisa here.
Kusvika patisingafungidzire tingasvike,

Pakubata hwaro hwehunhu hwedu.
Tinotendera munzvimbo iyi,
Inoita kuti tisangane.

Asi iyezvino mukadzi uyo anokuunganidzazve,
Kuhupenyu hwako hwekare, kubango-
Rohupenyu hwanezuro, achikushungurudza kuti uende.
Uye iwe, unofanirwa kuenda.
Kunge kupfuura kweshavi, kunge Svikiro-
Kunge zviroto, unorota.
Ucharota zvakare.
Uchatsveedzera muzviroto zvako izvi.
Uye hauchafi wakamukazve.

Shuviro yako iyi iri-
yokuti uchagara kure naye-
Uchichengetedza upenyu hwako muninga.
Unoramba kana kumbofunga nezvako,
uchagara kure naye-
Kunge mvura mugore renzara.
Kuti ugoona chete kamwenje kake nechekure-
Kachichenesa matenga.

Uchinyudza mufananidzo wezvirota zvako mugoridhe.
Muzviroto izvi unotsveedzerera, unokotsirira,
Unonyunguduka mumubvuri wezviroto zvako.
Uye unobvunuka mauri, kuchururukira pasi,
Kutambarara kubva mauri, kutandira-
Kuvirukira muhutsihutsi wehusiku.
Hwasvibisisa, mugurokuro rarodema rakashama.

Rudo rwako naye rwafashama,
Neropa dema romwoyo wako.
Urwo runodhonza tambo hombe,

163

Idzo dzomwoyo wako, uchiteerera, uchishuvira-
Kunzwa mhinduro-
Yemvura, iri pasi pamatombo matema-
Okutyisa, kuri mumwoyo mako.
Kuri kunyura kudzika pasi perwizi-
Rwomwoyo wako rurikuhwandiswa pasi.
Kunge rurikuenda pasi pasi panyika.
Kunge matombo apasipasi egungwa.

Hwezvero idzi, dzisingaperi kunge-
Madonhwe emvura, nzira yako yaakutsveedzerera.
Kuenda kusingaonekwi, unotumira tsamba yomumhepo-
Yomwoyo wako kuenda kuchitsuva,
Chokunyarara kwake, asi hapana kana donhwe-
Rokurova kwehana yako richirikurarama-
Mukati memwoyo wako, kunze kwehwezvero idzi.
Dzinoyambukira newe kumatunhu okushushikana norushayo.

164

These intimations
Tendai Rinos Mwanaka

She is touching you again
Touch being all of your sight
You step so carefully, so afraid
Of another deep and empty fall
Inwards into another void
If you knock her off-balance
Afraid of grabbing her
Too hard, lingering on the memory
Of why you are still there

Loitering together in the small hours
Holding onto the ropes of tenderness
Trying to reach those glistening
Beaches in each other's hearts
Two moonlit people, you face
Each other, fingers reaching out
Lost in the forests of your delights
Stroking each other's cheeks
Dressing each other with
The clothes of your need.

So much love and
Too many things to do with it
You both love, it seems
From abandonment and need
Perhaps silent, the consolation
Is, not being loved but
Rather you would love
Such extraordinary range
Touching your very human core

You believe in this range
For you to meet.

But she is now gathering you again
To your past, the flagpole of
Your past, asking you to go
And you, you have to go
Like a passing spirit, a genie
Like a dream; you dream
You will dream
You will sip through your dream
And you won't wake up

Your ambition is this
You will stay away
Keeping your secrets hidden
You have to feel nothing
You will stay away
Like rains in the drought year
So that you can only see her light
Brightening up the skies

Casting your image in gold
In the dream you slip, you sleep
Dissolve into its silhouette
And empty out again, bleeding
Spreading yourself out, speeding
Embroider yourself in the effete
Of darkness, in its blackening gullet

Your love is now filled with
The dark blood of your heart
That pulls the heavy ropes
Of your heart, listening, hoping

To hear the answer of
Water, beneath those black
Rocks of fear, in your heart
Sinking to the river bed
Of your heart, disappearing down
It seems into subduction zones
Like oceanic rocks

These intimations, endless as
Raindrops, your road slipping
Away unnoticed. You email
Your heart out to the island
Of her silences. But no dribble
Of your pulse will survive
In your heart, but these intimations.
Hovering in desolate horizons.

Nzvimbo yoRudo

Translation by Tendai Rinos Mwanaka

Dai mwoyo womurume uyu wairarama munyika yokunze kwawo, ko
ndezvipi zvisikwa zvokutanga zvinobatanidza kurarama uku?
Dai mwoyo wamukadzi uyu waiva mivara yetsito, muti wesipurusi,
nziyo, inisenzi, dandiro redandemutande, zviwanikwa zvasingaonekwi
kusimba kwazvo.
Rudo rwavo vaviri ava, uye makoronga anogaramaruri
anochengetedzwa muimba yakavakwa nezvisinakusimba.
Kunge miti zvainonzwa zvikuru kana kuchinaya, kuchipfunhapfunha...

Mashizha ruswiswi emiti mumvura tete tete iri kukosorera murufaro.
Kurira kwehana yohupenyu hwamakore anotambirira mumvura iyi.
Zvakangofanana nokudzikisira pasi kwakanaka kwerudo, kuita kunge
gumi ramakore mumaziso eshiri.
Apo madokazuva anosinirira mivari yeghoridhe uye kumbundikira
vaviri ava.
Uyu hupenyu hunotushuka nemufaro kupindidzira nomunerakasviba
ivhu renyika.

Dzimwe nguva maoko ake mukadzi uyu, ane kakuvhundukirira,
achitenderedza muviri womurume wake.
Dai ndaingogona kupinda mudendere rorwuoko rwake mukadzi
wangu!
Murume anotura befu zvinyoronyoro kunge hangaiwa.
Anogumbatira mukadzi uyu, kugumbatira nzvimbo dzose
dzechihwande dziripakati pavo.
Kubatana kwavo uku hupenyu chaihwo, idenga rawirira kunongoendwa
norudo chete.
Kushuvira kunogumbatira kwokupedzisira.
Varikubvumburudzana murudo urwu apo vakanamirira mukushamisisa
kwarwo.

Muviri worudo wakangofanana nenzvimbo yenzvimbo-
Muviri wenzvimbo wakangofanana nenzvimbo yorudo.
Mukadzi aripamusoro pegomo; anotarisira mudenga unjenjema-
Zuva rinovaimira parunako rwake mukadzi uyu,
Anosumudzira ruoko kune uyo wakasimudza maziso kwaari, kune
murume wake.

Ichokwadi ndezvakawandisisa, ichokwadi zviripesepese, ichokwadi
zvinogutsa mawungira enyika yavo iyi yorudo-
Nenziyo dzemazita omumwe nomumwe.
Kubvumirira kuri kuparanuka kwemiviri yavo kuri-
Kuseri kwezvinopihwa kubva munziyo yebonde ravo iri,
Inotapukirira muna, *mangwanani akanaka, ndinokudai!*

Ndivo avo, mumipanda yavo yenyama nyoro,
Vane ukasha, kukasikira, uye vatosvika vasati vasvika-
Pakuzivana pabonde iri, pakuziva rudo rwavo urwu.
Uye, kana miviri yavo yajairirana,
Kugutsikana kwavo nezvakavatenderedza kwakada kufanana
nokupengereka kunge kushambira mudenga risina mhepo.

Murume anonyatsowongorora mukadzi wake achiroverera sando
yezvaanofunga mundangariro dzake.
Kune kuda kuonesesa kurimukatikati kune vanhu, uko kuri mamaziso
memukadzi uyu,
Kana vanhu ava vasati varongonora meso avachapfeka pakutarisa kune
nyika.
Kufemereka kushoma munguva iyi, kunyoronyoro, kunoshamisisa.
Uye, zhowezhowe yakanyorovera ravanongonzwa chete nderehana
dzavo dzirikutindingura ngoma mukati mavo.
Runyararo ruchisunganidza mawungira aya erudo.

Mukadzi uyu anorara nomurume uyu, kuti ataure nechimupanze
chirimubako iri chonotodzesera humunhu.

Kudzidzisana nezvemakavi, anoita zvinhu zvivesunganidzo?
Zvinogona kudambuka nokuwondomoka.
Kumutsidzira kuda kuonesesa sekunge ndiyo keyi inovhurira zvese.
Kushuvirirana kwavo kwakangofanana umwe nomumwe.

Mukadzi uyu haisiri shamwari yomurume uyu chete, ndiye hana yake,
ndiye iye chaiye.
Kumurume uyu, hupenyu hwaiva pokurarira, hwindo, uye shamwari
yashanya-
Mushure mokunge asati asangana naye mukadzi uyu.
Murume uyu aiwa baba uye mai.
Mukadzi uyu ndiye baba namai vake.
Kunge mvura isina ubaba nohumai, rudo chete!

Vanobvumidza mwoyo yavo kushaya zvinoidzora kunyangwe painenge
yakanyarara,
Inotsvaga nziyo yemumwe nomumwe munazvakahwandiswa.
Murimo mumba munogara mwoyo zuvanezuva?
Ko chii chinonzi marwadzo apa?
Chii chaicho chinonzi marwadzo munzvimbo iyi yorudo?

****

*Twunhu twunoramba twakavasunganidza kuva tyiso mukusangana nezvinoda
kuvapa mazita ezvinotyisa, nyama dzinotyisa, mhuka dzinotyisa, kutyisidzirana
mumwe nomumwe!*

PLACE OF LOVE
Tendai Rinos Mwanaka

If his heart was reliant on the outside world then what primal
materials would make up this reliance
Her heart is a weave of charcoal, blue spruce, hymns, incense,
Spider's silk; materials hardly seen as fortress
Their love, and the hallows that live within it is best housed in a loose
weave
Like woods would feel best when it is raining, barely raining…

The green leaves of trees in the rain fluttering and sneezing in
happiness
A life-throb of ages dancing, in the rain
Is love's low cascade, a decade in a bird's eyes
As evening flows in and around them
It's a life that shoots in joy through the dirty of the earth

Sometimes her hands, in panicky, all over him
If he can nestle into her palms
He sighs up like a turtle dove
As he coves her, the secret places between them
Their lovemaking; it is life, it is the sky falling where only love can go
It is a desire that embraces the margins
They are fumbling on love as they are stuck in the shock of it

The graph of love is like the place of space
The graph of space is like the place of love
She is on top of the mountain; she looks up at the wonderful sky
The sun beams on her beauty
She waves down at those who look up to her, at him

Obviously its possibilities, obviously everywhere, obviously feeding
their humming spheres

With the music of each other's names
Admitting how spasmodic their bodies are
Beyond the given over music of orgasm
Twirls in, *good morning, I love you.*

There are, in their soft containers
They are rough, rapid and ready
To figure out each other, to figure out love
And, when their bodies are orientated
Satisfaction with the surroundings is almost psychical as swimming in
no wind

He watches her jack hammering notes into her memory
At the curious inward look people would have, that's in her eyes
When they have not yet formed a face they will wear to look out on the
world
The breathlessness of that moment, small, wondrous
And, the only noise is made by their hearts beating
Silence yoking love's toll

She sleeps with him, to speak to the ape whose hibernation habours
humanity
Teaching each other about the strings, which makes things strings?
That fray and tangle
Turning on curiosity as a passkey
Their longing equals each other's longings

She is not just his friend; she is his heart, himself
For him, life was a bed, a window, a friend come visiting
Before he met her
He is now of father and mother
She is the father and mother
Like water, it is love

Allowing their hearts no hindrance even when they are silent
They still sound each other's smells in secret
Which was always heart's home?
What is pain?
What is really pain in this place of love?

****

*The things that keep them menacing enough in the face of what aims
to name them menacing things, menacing meat, menacing animals, menacing each
other?*

Ljubav iz trinaeste galaksije
Ivan Gaćina

U plavičastom sazviježđu,
na pragu slavoluka vremena,
tražim ostatke prošlosti
među milijardama zvijezda.
Krhotke prohujale ljubavi
griju hladnoću svemira
preko lunarnih sjena
i kozmomliječnih staza.
Na vremenskoj ljuljačci
njišem se kroz svjetlosne godine
tražeći tvoje nježno lice
skriveno iza magličastog platna
ondje gdje atomi i kvanti
pod mističnim kupolama,
kršeći zakone refleksije,
kreiraju kaskade zrcalnog postojanja.
U kraljevstvu iza crnih rupa
iščezavaju moje rastočene boli,
uvirući kroz spiralne hodnike
u zlatnu dolinu kozmoumlja.
Kroz vatreno praskozorje,
slijedim poput lovca tragove tvoje duše,
sakupljajući moje raspršene čežnje,
paramparčad iz trinaeste galaksije.

Love From the Thirteenth Galaxy
Translation by Ivan Gaćina

In the bluish constellation,
on the threshold of the triumphal arch of time,
I search for the remnants of the past
among milliards of stars.
The shards of the bygone love
warm the coldness of the universe
through the lunar shadows
and cosmic-milky pathways.
I swing on the time swing
through the light years
looking for your gentle face
hidden behind a hazy canvas
there where atoms and quanta
under the mystical domes,
violating the laws of reflection,
create the cascades of mirror existence.
In the kingdom behind the black holes
my dissolved pains disappear,
flowing through the spiral corridors
into the golden valley of the cosmosmind.
Through the fiery dawn,
like a hunter, I follow the traces of your soul,
collecting my scattered longings,
the shards from the thirteenth galaxy.

Srcosilnice praskozorja
Ivan Gaćina

U besanoj dolini, ispod rašljaste lune
plesali smo valcer predvođen rapsodijom
preko razlistanih trenutaka međuzvježđa
okolorićenih kumkumom.

Sjeme mudrosti posađeno u našim srcima
razdanjivalo je strasti
koje su uzburkale osjećaje
dok su se njene usne stapale u nirvanu.

Kroz odraze smrznutih uspomena
razbili smo nerazrješive kodove
zarobljene nitima kozmogordijskog čvora
ulazeći u ekstazu ugaslog svjetoumlja.

Uramljene kišnim kapljicama ljubavi,
iz nektara božanstvene ambrozije
emocije su prošle pokraj fulgentne nade
kroz žarište krstarećih snoviđenja.

Dijamantno praskozorje od pikantnih srcosilnica
stopljeno je u njenim očima
koje uranjaju u sjajokazje blaženstva
preko jaza premošćenog eufonijom.

Heart Forces of the Daybreak

Translation by Ivan Gaćina

In a sleepless valley, below the forked moon
we danced the waltz to the rhapsody
across the interstellar leafy moments
painted with kumkuma.

The seeds of wisdom planted in our hearts
awoke the passions
stirring our feelings
while her lips melted into nirvana.

Through the reflections of frozen memories
we broke the unsolvable codes
trapped by threads of the cosmogordian knot
entering the ecstasy of an extincted worldview.

Framed by the raindrops of love,
from the nectar of divine ambrosia
emotions passed by in the fulgent hope
through the focus of cruising visions.

A diamond daybreak from spicy heart forces
is drowned in her eyes
immersing into glossy guides of bliss
across the gap bridged by euphony.

Vivaldijeva savršena gramatika
Ivan Gaćina

Dozivao sam te kroz maglu,
između nesvršenih glagola i misaonih imenica,
kako bi mi mogla detaljno objasniti
tajnu gramatiku kozmotantričke ljubavi.
Krivudajući putem
koji vodi ka džungli trokutastog oblika
preko rijeke Lete,
točke i zareze prevrtao sam ti u krilu
dok sam splavario na valovima samospoznaje i samosvijesti
da ne bih potonuo u izgubljenom vremenu.
Obilazeći meandre sirovih bjelina,
pomno sam proučavao bespuća
između elipse i uskličnika
kako bih mogao razvrstati epitete i atribute
pomiješane sa zbrkanom interpunkcijom
na proplanku čežnje.
Dok sam mislio da te čitam kao otvorenu knjigu,
osmjehnula si se zagonetno
kad si me namamila, između fragmenata,
u ćorsokak (ne)dovršene balade
(ili možda pustolovnog romana).
Koristeći upitnike za sastavljanje kozmičkog tkiva
i kotrljajući sudbinu međuprostora
prema Vivaldijeva Četiri godišnja doba,
mudrost iz neistraženih, zrcalnih rječnika
lebdjela je onkraj nevidljivih navodnika
spajajući praznine između elipsi
u (ne)zatvorenim vitičastim zagradama.

Vivaldi's Perfect Grammar
Translation by Ivan Gaćina

I called you through fog,
among imperfect verbs and abstract nouns,
so that you could detaily explain me
the secret grammar of cosmos tantric love.
Traveling along a zig-zag road
that leads to a triangular-shaped jungle
across the river Lethe,
I turned dots and commas in your lap
as I rafted on the waves of self-knowledge and self-awareness
so as not to sink into lost time.
Touring the meanders of raw whites,
I carefully studied the wilderness
between an ellipsis and an exclamation mark
so that I could classify epithets and attributes
mixed with confused punctuation
on a longing glade.
As I thought I could read you like an open book,
you smiled enigmatically
when you lured me, between the fragments,
to a dead end of an (un)completed ballad
(or perhaps an adventure novel).
Using question marks to assemble the cosmic tissue
and rolling the destiny of the interspace
to the Vivaldi's Four Seasons,
the wisdom from unexplored, mirror dictionaries
hovered beyond the invisible quotation marks
connecting the gaps between the ellipses
in the (un)closed curly braces.

U kolijevci moga srca
Ivan Gaćina

U mome su srcu neistraženi svjetovi
koji plove u smjeru trodimenzionalne kazaljke sata
dok ih povjetarac očarava mjesečevim prahom
kojeg je oteo kad je uzburkao ocean ljubavi.

U njemu su također ispričane i neispričane priče,
a dijelimo ih kada se nađemo na istoj stazi
i kada se borimo protiv vjetrenjača ovog iluzornog života
kojeg zilijuni nebeskih krijesnica nose u budućnost.

Dok me hrani snažnim vanvremenim izrazima,
ono sjedi na pijedestalu poetske moći,
a pri zvonjavi crkvenih zvona sjaji poput sunca
i obdaruje me čudesnim osjećajima.

Odano mi je čak i onda kada se igram sa svojom sudbinom,
a dok prolazim kroz dubinske magle očaja i depresije,
ono se spušta kako bi mi zaštitilo bolnu Ahilovu petu
pri čemu sakuplja moje uspomene u ogromnu škrinju empatije.

Pomoću razgranatih kozmičkih silnica ono ziba lađu života
kako bih na mirnim valovima bezbrižno mogao provesti svoj cilj,
a povremeno kroz tišinu tone u tajanstveni miris ruža,
i kad boje duge lutaju kroz moje oči ono upija nijanse ljepote.

U mojem je srcu Kupidova zalutala strelica
koja me uči kako da ispunim svoje snove
i da najlakše svladavam prepreke u mom životu
dok rijeka blaženstva priče iz njegove kolijevke odnosi u beskraj.

In the Cradle of My Heart
Translation by Ivan Gaćina

There are unexplored worlds in my heart
which sail in the three-dimensional clockwise direction
while the breeze enchants them with moon dust
which he seized while stirring the ocean of love.

Told and untold stories are also in it,
and we share them when we find ourselves on the same track
and when we tilt at windmills of this illusory life
carried by zillions of celestial fireflies into the future.

As it feeds me with powerful timeless expressions,
it sits on the poetic power pedestal,
and when church bells ring, it shines like the sun
and endows me with magical feelings.

It's loyal to me even when I play with my destiny,
and as I pass through the deep mists of despair and depression,
it comes down to protect my painful Achilles heel
whereby it gathers my memories in a huge chest of empathy.

With the help of branched cosmic forces, it shakes the boat of life
so that I could carelessly pursue my goal on peaceful waves,
and it occasionally sinks through the silence into the mysterious scent
of roses
and when rainbow colors wander through my eyes, it absorbs the
shades of beauty.

In my heart is Cupid's stray arrow
which teaches me how to fulfill my dreams
and to most easily overcome obstacles in my life
as the river of bliss carries its cradle stories into infinity.

Zvjezdani plašt ljubavi
Ivan Gaćina

Da sam kozmički električar,
od zvjezdane tkanine satkao bih plašt ljubavi,
oplemenjen nitima lave (da razbudim beskrajni ocean),
i ušio znakove poznatih i nepoznatih pisama
koja su zmajevi otpuhali u carstvo s druge strane planine
kako bi zavladala harmonija između svjetova.
Dodao bih livadne boje u smjesu budućnosti
da boemski umjetnik može oslikati dubinu moje mašte
na oltaru gdje se život i neživot prepliću između bljeskova,
a čarobni prah bacio bih u deltu Nila
kako bi moglo narasti džinovsko stablo spoznaje dobra i zla.
Nad plaštom ljubavi, sjaj tisuću sunaca obasjao bi optičara
koji prekraja svjetonazor pomoću endogenih i egzogenih sila
dok nebo presvlači svoje jutarnje ruho,
a kad se zemlja zarotira oko nadnaravne grafitno-kristalne osi,
matematičar bi priključio krila logike
kako bi nas oktalni brod mogao provesti kroz sudbinu.
Kad bi ljudi znali upravljati snovima,
plaštovi ljubavi zamijenili bi nebeski i zemni promet
dok bi se spoznaje s druge strane zrcala raspršile u svakodnevlje,
a vrtlar bi koristio biljni sat s aurora borealis efektima
kako bi cvijeće moglo stvarati poentilistički oslikane stihove
koje smaragdni leptiri nose iznad tišine oceana.
Posijao bih sjeme mudrosti na skrivene planinske proplanke
da donese neobično i mistično voće s dalekih planeta,
a ostatak zvjezdane tkanine bacio bih u vjetar iluzije
kako bi se magnetski polovi mogli zarotirati u smjeru ljubavi,
gdje je zidar zabetonirao kamena srca mitskih gradova.

A Starry Mantle of Love
Translation by Ivan Gaćina

If I were a cosmic electrician,
I would make a mantle of love from the starry fabric,
enriched with threads of lava (to wake an endless ocean),
and I would sew together the signs of known and unknown letters
blown away by dragons into the empire on the other side of the
mountain
to bring harmony between the worlds.
I would add meadow colors to the mixture of the future
so that a bohemian artist can paint the depths of my imagination
on the altar where life and non-life intertwine between flashes,
and I would throw magic dust in the Nile delta
so that a giant tree of the knowledge of good and evil could grow.
Above the love mantle, the glow of a thousand suns would illuminate
an optician
reshaping the worldview with endogenous and exogenous forces
while the sky changes its morning attire,
and when the earth rotates around the supernatural graphite-crystal
axis,
the mathematician would join the wings of logic
so that the octal ship could guide us through destiny.
If people knew how to manage their dreams,
the love mantles would replace traffic in the heaven and on earth
while cognitions on the other side of the mirror would scatter into
everyday life,
and the gardener world use a herbal clock with aurora borealis effects
so that flowers could create pointillistically painted verses,
carried by the emerald butterflies above the silence of the ocean.
I would sow the seeds of wisdom on the hidden mountain glades
to bear unusual and mystical fruit from distant planets,
and I would throw the rest of the starry fabric into the wind of illusion
so that the magnetic poles could rotate in the direction of love,

where the mason concreted the stone hearts of mythical cities.

Mmap Multi-disciplinary Series

If you have enjoyed *Love Notes: Everything is Love, An Anthology of Africa and East European Indigenous Languages, Vol 1* consider these other fine books in the **Multi-disciplinary Series** from *Mwanaka Media and Publishing:*

Africanization and Americanization Anthology Volume 1, Searching for Interracial, Interstitial, Intersectional and Interstates Meeting Spaces, Africa Vs North America by Tendai R Mwanaka
A Conversation..., A Contact by Tendai Rinos Mwanaka
Africa, UK and Ireland: Writing Politics and Knowledge Production Vol 1 by Tendai R Mwanaka
Writing Language, Culture and Development, Africa Vs Asia Vol 1 by Tendai R Mwanaka, Wanjohi wa Makokha and Upal Deb
Zimbolicious: An Anthology of Zimbabwean Literature and Arts, Vol 3 by Tendai Mwanaka
Drawing Without Licence by Tendai R Mwanaka
Writing Grandmothers/ Escribiendo sobre nuestras raíces: Africa Vs Latin America Vol 2 by Tendai R Mwanaka and Felix Rodriguez
Tiny Human Protection Agency by Megan Landman
Ghetto Symphony by Mandla Mavolwane
A Portrait of Defiance by Tendai Rinos Mwanaka
Nationalism: (Mis)Understanding   Donald Trump's Capitalism, Racism, Global Politics, International Trade and Media Wars, Africa Vs North America Vol 2 by Tendai R Mwanaka
Ouafa and Thawra: About a Lover From Tunisia by Arturo Desimone
Zimbolicious: An Anthology of Zimbabwean Literature and Arts, Vol 4 by Tendai Mwanaka and Jabulani Mzinyathi
Chitungwiza Mushamukuru Anthology by Tendai Mwanaka
The Day and the Dweller: A Study of the Emerald Tablets by Jonathan Thompson
Zimbolicious: An Anthology of Zimbabwean Literature and Arts, Vol 5 by Tendai Mwanaka

Robotics Anthology, Africa vs Asia Vol 2 by Tendai Rinos Mwanaka

Soon to be released

Shaping Up by Tendai Rinos Mwanaka

https://facebook.com/MwanakaMediaAndPublishing/

Printed in the United States
by Baker & Taylor Publisher Services